Six Keys to Creating the Life You Desire

STOP PURSUING THE UNATTAINABLE AND
FIND THE FULFILLMENT YOU TRULY NEED

MITCH MEYERSON
& LAURIE ASHNER

New Harbinger Publications, Inc.

Publisher's Note

This publication is designed to provide accurate and authoritative information in regard to the subject matter covered. It is sold with the understanding that the publisher is not engaged in rendering psychological, financial, legal, or other professional services. If expert assistance or counseling is needed, the services of a competent professional should be sought.

Distributed in the U.S.A. by Publisher's Group West; in Canada by Raincoast Books; in Great Britain by Airlift Book Company, Ltd.; in South Africa by Real Books, Ltd.; in Australia by Boobook; and in New Zealand by Tandem Press.

Copyright © 1999 Mitch Meyerson
      New Harbinger Publications, Inc.
      5674 Shattuck Avenue
      Oakland, CA 94609

Cover design by SHELBY DESIGNS & ILLUSTRATES.
Edited by Kayla Sussell.
Typeset by Tracy Marie Powell.

Library of Congress Catalog Card Number: 98-67408.
ISBN 1-57224-125-X Paperback

Printed in the United States of America.

New Harbinger Publications' Website address: www.newharbinger.com

First printing

To Jay,

For your inspiration, enthusiasm and encouragement.
Most of all for lighting the path by living the life you desire.

—Mitch and Laurie

Contents

Table of Self-Help Questionnaires   **vii**

Preface   **ix**

Acknowledgments   **xi**

1 The Mystery of Chronic Dissatisfaction   **1**

2 When You Can't Relax   **21**
The Key: Trust

3 When Nothing Makes You Happy for Long   **55**
The Key: Affirmation

4 When You Can't Stop Comparing Yourself to Other People   **89**
The Key: Identity

5 When You Can't Achieve the Success You Desire   **123**
The Key: Competence

6 When You Can't Find the Right Person   **157**
The Key: Intimacy

7 When You Can't Find Meaning in Your Life   **187**
The Key: Purpose

8 Creating Change: Getting the Results You Want   **211**

9 Designing the Life of Your Dreams   **223**

Resources   **243**

Suggested Reading   **245**

References   **247**

List of Self-Help Questionnaires

	Chapter
Are You Chronically Dissatisfied?	1
The Key Issues Inventory	1
Measuring Your General Level of Anxiety	2
What's the Price You Pay for Never Being Able to Relax?	2
Are You Compulsively Self-Reliant?	2
What Do You Really Need?	2
Measuring Your General Level of Anhedonia (Joylessness)	3
The Depressive Retreat from Feelings	3
Are You a Problem-Focused Thinker?	3
Creating More Happiness in Your Life	3
Taking Your Emotional Inventory	3
Identifying Your Family Secrets	4
How Competitive Did You Have to Be in School?	4
Finding Yourself	4
Were You Overparented?	5
The Entitlement Quiz	5
Are You Demand-Resistant?	5

The Relationship Questionnaire   **6**

The Intimacy Inventory   **6**

How Do You Distance People?   **6**

Do You Feel Your Life Has Purpose?   **7**

The Scarcity/Abundance Quiz   **7**

How Giving Are You?   **7**

Preface

Many of us spend our lives pursuing the shadow but not the substance of our desires. We seek the fantasies and dreams that promise relief from old pain, chasing what's unattainable or just plain wrong for us. The struggle brings up nagging questions: *Why can't I relax? Why am I never happy for long? Why do I keep comparing myself to others?* The answer, in part, is that unattainable fantasies provide a brief, unsatisfying excitement that saps motivation for doing anything real. Fantasies about unavailable people, unachievable ambitions, money, fame, and freedom are often serious addictions. And once addicted, we suffer enormous emptiness (withdrawal) when we can't have them.

It is possible to create a life that's authentic and reflects who you truly want to be—a life of enthusiasm, focus, and meaning. But first you need to deal with the key issues that block such a quest: Trust, Affirmation, Identity, Competence, Intimacy, and Purpose. These are big words and big concepts. But there is no reason to feel overwhelmed. This easy-to-use workbook contains effective action plans for discovering and breaking through the six key blocks that undermine your search for satisfaction. Through the use of diagnostic questionnaires and many strategically designed exercises, you will be able to identify your key issues, learn how your old patterns are keeping you stuck, and create new choices.

If you have been working and reaching for goals, yet find that every achievement seems ephemeral; if you feel a hunger that your dreams only seem to magnify; if you are longing for a life that is rich yet has a quiet center of calm, this book will be an important guide. Here is a map for locating the place where true satiety becomes possible.

This workbook is a highly useful tool for therapists as well as self-help readers. The inventories and strategic exercises will be a welcome addition to any treatment program that is focused on enhancing life satisfaction. The book offers clients an opportunity to work systematically during the week on critical issues, and then bring the fruits of those efforts back into the therapy hour.

This is a book that can make a real difference, that can finally explain why we so often struggle without reaching fulfillment, and how we can finally break through the obstacles to our deepest desires.

—Matthew McKay, Ph.D.
author of *Self-Esteem*

Special thanks to Matt McKay for believing in this project from the beginning and for sharing the "best meal ever" at Salvatories; Kayla Sussell, for the helpful suggestions and talented editing of this manuscript; the wonderful team at New Harbinger; my parents, Ed and Marion Meyerson for providing the opportunities that allow me to make creative choices; Corky, Larry, Pat, Amy, Shirley, Marvin, Bobby and George for their continued support; my collegues and friends, Ken Celiano, Howard Weissman, Cindy Mazura, Michelle DeCola, and Aimee Mooney for their creative energy; Gail and Howard at Transitions Bookstore for their amazing contribution to personal growth; Pam Berns and *Chicago Life* Magazine for supporting our writing over the past decade; my fellow musicians Chuck, Neil, George, Ron, Pete, Keith, June, Riki, Ed and Eric; and most of all to Laurie, who is my best friend, partner in adventure, and one amazing writer.

—Mitch Meyerson

Special thanks to my sister and brother-in-law, Marcie and Howard Tilkin—here's book number six, can you believe it?; Dr. Jerald Schwab, whose wisdom could definitely fill a book; Susan Piser, the therapist's therapist; my friends who put up with phone calls I don't return when I'm on a deadline and understand anyway, especially Ellie Sigel, Mary Wells, Carrie Worley, and Mark and Martha Rubenstein. Most of all, thank you Mitch for being the real key to everything I've ever desired.

—Laurie Ashner

The Mystery of Chronic Dissatisfaction

If I get this promotion, I'll be the happiest person on earth.

If I could lose five pounds, I'd be thrilled.

*When we save enough for a down payment and
move to a place of our own, I'll be satisfied.*

When I finally pass the real estate licensing exam, I'll be able to relax.

*If we had the money so I could quit my job and stay
home with my kids, I'd never ask for another thing.*

Is This Book for You?

Sound familiar? The people who made these statements went on to achieve the goals they had set for themselves. They got exactly what they wanted. But, somehow, when they got what they wanted, they found that it still wasn't enough. *Six Keys to Creating the Life You Desire* is a workbook for people who have met many of their goals, but who still feel a nagging sense of dissatisfaction with themselves and their lives.

This book is about men like Steve, who was obsessed with becoming a partner in a major law firm. He worked eighty-hour weeks and filed thousands of billable hours. However, when he was finally made a partner, his happiness faded faster than a summer tan. Nowadays, he thinks, "Maybe I should have been a prosecutor, that would have been something important."

It's about women like Evelyn, an artist who invented children's toys. She beat her head against the closed doors of gift shops and department stores for ten years before a venture capital firm agreed to finance her business. "I should be ecstatic," she says, "but I can't stop worrying. What if my toys hit the market and sink like stones?"

It's about Carl, with a career he enjoys, children he adores, a new home, and a growing feeling of depression; Alice, recently engaged, who suddenly feels something is "missing" in her relationship; Mark, who has changed jobs six times in the last three years; and Candice who wonders why she spends thousands of dollars on clothes and makeup and still can't stand the way she looks.

This workbook is *not* about perfectionists, although perfectionists will clearly see themselves in much of it. It is about people who, no matter what they have and no matter how hard they struggled to get it, feel little sense of fulfillment.

As therapists, we can assure you that many people seek treatment for feelings of emptiness or mild depression. The clinical term for this feeling is *dysthymia*, which means chronic low-grade depression. We've spent more than ten years doing clinical work and research with people suffering from chronic discontent and dysthymia. We wanted to know why some people get exactly what they want in life, and still end up disappointed. We also wondered, why do others find it impossible to choose the right career, or the right relationship? Why do so many people crave the one thing they can never have?

We also discovered people who are satisfied with their lives in spite of many problems, failures, and conflicts. What do such satisfied people know that the rest of us don't? What is their secret to living fulfilled lives in the face of difficulties, stumbling blocks, and adversities?

We discovered that the "there is never-enough" mindset bears little or no connection to what you have or don't have. We were able to isolate the reasons why many people find the road to satisfaction so difficult. We learned that people who are never satisfied often set themselves up for disappointment unconsciously, and there are startling reasons why they do that. (We published these findings in *When Is Enough, Enough? What You Can Do If You Never Feel Satisfied* (Meyerson and Ashner 1996). Since then many people have asked us if there were more exercises and concrete steps they could work through. That was where the idea for this workbook was born.

If you think that dissatisfaction and a "never-enough" mindset are relevant to your life, but you are still not sure whether this book is for you, let us suggest that you take a look at the following questionnaire.

Are You Chronically Dissatisfied?

Many of us are all-or-nothing, black-or-white thinkers who feel overwhelmed when tackling such a question as, "Am I happy?" We tend to say, "Yes, I am happy" or "No, I'm unhappy," but all the while we know that neither answer is really correct. We know that the true answer lies somewhere between "yes" and "no," but we don't know what to do with such a "gray" area. So, the first step is to take a good look into the gray areas.

The quiz that follows will help you to examine the gray parts of your life and to quantify your feelings.

Questionnaire

Read each statement and put an X in the appropriate box (0 = never, 1 = rarely, 2 = sometimes, 3 = often, 4 = always)

	0	1	2	3	4
1. When I succeed at something, I don't feel much joy. It makes me wonder, "Can I do it again?"					
2. I vacillate between feeling talented and special and then wondering, "Who do I think I am?"					
3. I feel my efforts aren't recognized enough, yet compliments make me feel uncomfortable.					
4. I focus on the negative aspects of a situation more than the positive ones.					
5. I don't believe it's enough to be just average. Being average makes me feel like a failure.					
6. I take more than my share of the blame for what goes wrong in relationships, at work, and in my family.					
7. I am drawn to situations that compel me to prove myself to others.					
8. I minimize the anxiety and depression I feel because I'm so used to it. It feels like the true me.					
9. I find it hard to reach out to others for support.					
10. I feel I can't stop striving to be better, but I rarely get where I want to be, so I'm often emotionally frustrated.					
11. I tend to get very excited about a new car, new suit, new piece of jewelry, etc., and then I tire of it quickly.					
12. I've had several relationships where I was head over heels at first, and then it turned into pick, pick, pick, and nothing the other person could do pleased me.					
13. I definitely see myself as underpaid.					
14. I tend to think of what could go wrong instead of what's going well.					

Scoring: Add up the numbers in the boxes you checked.

Scoring

0–14: You have an excellent capacity to feel satisfied, appreciate what you have, and to express your own unique voice in the world.

15–25: You are basically satisfied, but you will find information in this book that will help you to identify subtle blocks to self-fulfillment and to take concrete steps toward creating even more satisfaction in your life.

26–41: You have tendencies toward chronic dissatisfaction. The exercises in this workbook should help you to discover the cause of those tendencies and to create new options for yourself.

42 and above: This score indicates a pervasive pattern of chronic dissatisfaction. You don't need to live with it forever. The material in this workbook will provide you with concrete directions for achieving greater satisfaction.

How to Get the Most from This Workbook

Chronic dissatisfaction doesn't have to be a life sentence. This book offers you a combination of user-friendly self-assessment questionnaires, psychological explorations for your presenting problems, and carefully designed personal growth exercises to create change in your life. Think of them as the keys that will unlock the best self within yourself.

Begin with The Key Issues Inventory in the next section, "What's Really Missing? Identifying Your Key Issues." This simple inventory will help you to determine which chapters will be most beneficial for you. You will learn to assess and chart your issues graphically so that you will be able to visualize where you need to focus. Your answers to this inventory will guide you to your own individualized treatment program.

Next go to the specific chapters indicated by your Key Issues Inventory. These will be chapters 3 through 8. You may not need to work through all of these chapters. Most people relate strongly to three or four of the core issues. Work through the chapters that have the information that is the most relevant to your personal issues. Finally, work through the sentence completion exercises in chapter 9, "Designing the Life of Your Dreams," to create a vision of a life that will be the most fulfilling one you can imagine.

While you are working through the exercises, keep this in mind: Books are a wonderful source of information. They can illuminate important connections between our personal histories and our current struggles. The insights gained through books can be very stimulating. But insight alone does not necessarily create change in our lives.

Over the years we have worked with many clients who could analyze themselves with great precision. Yet with all of their theoretical knowledge they were stuck repeating the same patterns—over and over. Knowledge alone is not curative. The formula for change is insight *plus action*. You may be tempted to read through the exercises rather than to do them. You are not alone if you are reluctant to put pencil to paper on such heartfelt issues. You will, however, make the most progress if you actually do the work instead of just reading about it. We guarantee it.

What's Really Missing?
Identifying Your Key Issues

We shall not cease from exploration
And the end of all our exploring
Will be to arrive where we started
And know the place for the first time.

—T. S. Eliot, "The Four
Quartets, Little Giddings, V"

Do you always feel that something is missing? That thought need not be so depressing. Such feelings can be a wake-up call. They can give you the energy to move forward to create new experiences, goals, and dreams. They can help you change what isn't working in your life. They can lead to a renewed sense of purpose and ambition. Unfortunately, they can also make you feel frustrated and powerless.

How can you use your dissatisfaction to create a results-oriented action plan whereby you can create greater happiness, contentment, and fulfillment in your life? The first step is to take a clear look at what's causing you to feel dissatisfied. That is the purpose of this chapter.

Your answers to The Key Issues Inventory that follows will allow you to identify which chapters in this workbook will be the most useful for you. It contains statements divided into eight groups. Each statement represents a core belief about life. To complete the inventory, score each statement in a numerical range from 1 to 9 with "strongly disagree" ranked as 1 and "strongly agree" ranked as 9. The more honest you can be, the more feedback you will receive.

The Key Issues Inventory

Assign a number that best describes how you feel concerning each of the following statements. Base your answers on what has been true for you for the greater part of your life.

Strongly Disagree	Mildly Disagree	Neutral	Mildly Agree	Strongly Agree
0 1	2 3	4 5	6 7	8 9

Group 1 *24*	Score
1. I find it easy to relax.	*3*
2. I would describe myself as a happy person.	*6*
3. When I'm hurt, mad, sad, or happy I know it. I can easily identify my emotions.	*6*
4. I pride myself on my perseverance; I complete projects.	*8*
5. Love is an easy emotion to express.	*4*

	Score
6. I am clear about what I want in life and I have definite plans for my future.	2
Group 2 92	**Score**
1. I find it difficult to ask for help.	4
2. I often focus on and think about my problems.	6
3. I don't really know what I want or what would make me happy.	6
4. I don't think of myself as successful.	5
5. I think that if people knew the real me, they wouldn't like me.	1
6. I find myself going through life with little sense of direction or purpose.	0
Group 3 (14)	**Score**
1. I feel safe and at ease with my parents and siblings.	2 -
2. I know my strengths and I'm not reluctant to acknowledge them.	5 -
3. It's fairly easy for me to identify what I want and what I need.	2 -
4. I feel my parents helped me build self-confidence by encouraging me to take responsibility for my successes and failures.	2 -
5. My parents had a good marriage that I think of as a good model.	1
6. My family encouraged me to follow my own dreams and intuition.	1
Group 4 31	**Score**
1. I tend to worry a lot.	8
2. It is common for me to feel sad or blue.	4
3. I have often felt that it was not a good idea to speak my mind honestly and openly to my family.	2
4. I spend more time avoiding things than doing them.	6
5. I'm afraid of what people will think of me if they really knew me.	3
6. I find that my work often leaves me feeling unfulfilled.	8
Group 5 20	**Score**
1. I find it easy to rely on others.	0
2. I make a conscious effort to do things that I love to do.	6
3. I have a strong sense of who I am.	4

	Score
4. I feel confident in my ability to make money.	6
5. I have several close intimate relationships.	4
6. I believe it's important to follow your passion and do what you really feel is meaningful with your life.	6
Group 6 21	**Score**
1. I find it scary to share my true thoughts and feelings with others.	5
2. My family tends to respond more when I have a problem than when I talk about something I've achieved.	3
3. I often compare myself with others.	7
4. In my childhood, a parent often rescued me when I struggled.	1
5. It's hard for me to be emotionally honest with people.	4
6. When I think about my future, I often feel depressed because nothing really excites me about moving forward.	9
Group 7 33	**Score**
1. I find it easy to delegate some responsibilities to others when necessary.	7
2. Each day I spend some time being grateful for what I have.	3
3. I usually trust my own thoughts and feelings.	7
4. I rarely look to others to save the day when I've messed up. I feel ultimately responsible for my mistakes.	9
5. I feel close to my parents and siblings.	3
6. I feel comfortable expressing my creative voice. I discuss ideas and thoughts even if they seem unusual.	4
Group 8 26	**Score**
1. My body often feels tense.	5
2. When people compliment me, I have a hard time believing they really mean it.	3
3. I'm not really clear about what would make me happy.	5
4. I often struggle to meet the deadlines I set for myself at work.	3
5. I have had difficulty finding a significant romantic partner	6
6. If I lived my life according to my true passion, I'm afraid people would disapprove.	4

MKII—Meyerson Key Issues Inventory © 1998

Scoring Your Inventory

The following table is designed to help you tabulate your scores. Record your answers to the questions in groups 1, 3, 5, and 7 exactly as they appear on your quiz.

For questions in groups 2, 4, 6, and 8, subtract your score from 10. For example, if you scored 3 on a question from an even-numbered group, you would enter a score of 7 (10–3 = 7).

After you enter all of your scores, add them up to get your total from each question.

	Question 1	Question 2	Question 3	Question 4	Question 5	Question 6
Group 1	3	6	6	8	4	2
Group 2 (reverse	4	6	6	5	1	0
Group 3	2	5	2	2	1	1
Group 4 (reverse)	8	4	2	6	3	8
Group 5	0	6	4	6	4	6
Group 6 (reverse)	5	3	7	1	4	1
Group 7	7	3	7	9	3	4
Group 8 (reverse)	5	7	5	3	6	4
TOTAL	34	36	39	40	26	40
	TRUST	AFFIRMATION	IDENTITY	COMPETENCE	INTIMACY	PURPOSE

What Do These Scores Mean?

In *When Is Enough, Enough?* (Meyerson and Ashner 1996), we identified some of the questions most often posed to us as therapists. These questions are:

- Why can't I just relax?

- Why is it that nothing makes me happy for long?

- Why can't I stop comparing myself to other people?

- Why don't I follow through on my dreams?

- Why can't I find the right person?

- Why can't I seem to find meaning in my life?

These are the Six Key Questions underlying chronic dissatisfaction. They are common areas of frustration for many of us. If we knew the answer to these questions, we'd have the key to creating the happier life we desire.

There is a key issue underlying the answer to each of these questions. Those "keys" are trust, affirmation, identity, competence, intimacy, and purpose. In other words, suppose you feel frustrated because no matter what you are experiencing, you can never let go and really enjoy yourself. Your *question* is, "Why can't I relax?" But the *key issue* is, "How much are you able to trust others or trust yourself?" And the questions that logically grow out of that question are, "Where does the notion that you must be in control and responsible at all times come from?" And "What can you do about it?"

The total of your scores (the bottom row) for each question will signify your composite score in the area of that core issue. For example: the total for column 1 equals you total score for TRUST. The column 2 total is your composite score for AFFIRMATION. In the same manner, the composite score for Question 3 = IDENTITY, Question 4 = COMPETENCE, Question 5 = INTIMACY, and Question 6 = PURPOSE.

What are your scores? We think of these as clues to the Key Issues Underlying Your Chronic Dissatisfaction.

Picture the key issues as a pyramid. Level One is the inner self. This part of our experience reflects our search for trust, affirmation, and identity. Like a house on a shaky foundation, if the "internal" issues of Level One are not resolved, they will affect Level Two, which is the interactive self. This level relates to how we interact with work and intimate relationships. Level Three reflects our search for purpose and spirituality and, in some disciplines, Level Three can be understood as the universal self.

What Does Your Chart Reveal?

John's Profile

John, forty-three, is a partner at a highly regarded advertising firm. He works an average of sixty hours a week and is envied by some of his colleagues for his perseverance and drive. What worries him about himself is his lack of success in his personal life. John

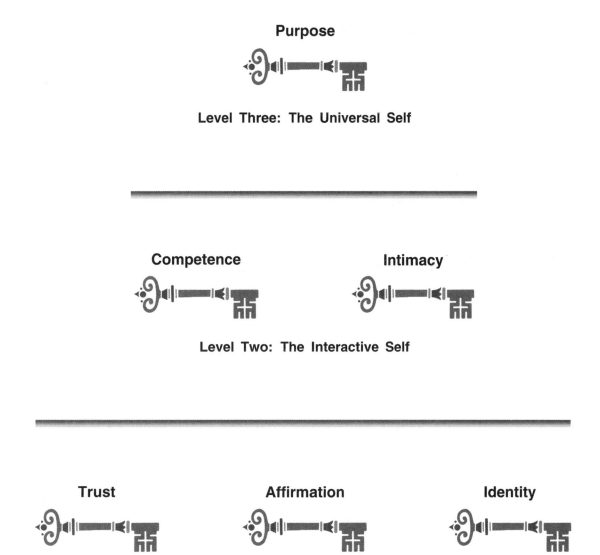

Figure 1.1   The Six Keys Underlying Chronic Dissatisfaction

has dated many women, but he has never stayed in one relationship for more than a year. He came into therapy discouraged. "I can't understand why I never seem to find the right woman," he said.

In therapy, John revealed that his father also worked long hours and rarely spent time with the family. He recalled his mother as a depressed semi-invalid who spent much of her time in bed. When his parents were home together, they would usually fight or spend their time in separate rooms. John felt that his mother looked to him for comfort and understanding, and he admitted that he often felt smothered, angry, and guilty because of his mother's neediness.

For John, his parents' marriage established a negative image of intimacy. Much like his father, the workplace for John has always been a place of solace, a source of validation and self-esteem. John's key issues profile can be seen below. He scores high on competence but the core of his dissatisfaction can be found with his issues regarding trust and intimacy.

John's Profile

	TRUST	AFFIRMATION	IDENTITY	COMPETENCE	INTIMACY	PURPOSE
55						
50						
45				▓		
40				▓		
35				▓		
30				▓		▓
25		▓		▓		▓
20		▓	▓	▓		▓
15		▓	▓	▓		▓
10		▓	▓	▓		▓
5	▓	▓	▓	▓		▓
0	▓	▓	▓	▓	▓	▓

Because John's major frustration is that he hasn't been able to develop a lasting relationship and has difficulty trusting other people to come through for him, the chapters he will get the most benefit from are chapter 2, "When You Can't Relax," and chapter 6, "When You Can't Find the Right Person."

Mary's Profile

Mary, thirty-four, is a wife and the mother of two children. She is a warm and caring person, a tower of strength. She gives her time and energy to the point of exhaustion. She came into therapy feeling depressed and empty, and unable to figure out why she felt that way.

As we began to explore her life, it became clear that her custom of dedicating herself to helping others was a lifelong pattern. She grew up in a dysfunctional family with a detached, alcoholic father and a mother who suffered from depression. Mary learned at a very early age that there was no one to attend to her needs and feelings. She became the family's caretaker, and grew up waiting on her mother and placating her father. She lived in constant fear and harbored many resentments, but to survive she became so detached from her emotions that she hardly knew that her chief emotions were fear and resentment.

Mary left home and got married at nineteen. In her own family she repeats the roles she developed and refined as a child: the strong one, the caretaker, the selfless one. On the surface her growing discontent was invisible, but in her thirties she became more and more depressed.

Mary's core issues are profiled on the next page. She appears to be actively involved with everyone she knows, and yet she scores low on intimacy. This is because she struggles so much with her own identity. How intimate can any of us feel with another if we can't really be ourselves with others?

Mary's Profile

	TRUST	AFFIRMATION	IDENTITY	COMPETENCE	INTIMACY	PURPOSE
55						
50						
45						
40						
35						
30						■
25					■	■
20				■	■	■
15		■		■	■	■
10	■	■		■	■	■
5	■	■		■	■	■
0	■	■	■	■	■	■

People with the same kind of family backgrounds that Mary has often have problems trusting other people because they are encouraged throughout childhood to rely on themselves and to meet their own needs as best they can. Although in Mary's case that encouraged her feelings of competence, she doesn't enjoy her life because she can never truly relax. The information in chapter 2, "When You Can't Relax," will be very helpful for Mary and those who need to learn how to be less compulsively self-reliant.

Mary will also find the information in chapter 4, "When You Can't Stop Comparing Yourself to Other People," important, as it deals with the struggle she and many other people have in understanding their identities.

Karl's Profile

Karl, twenty-four, is living at home with his parents and is attempting to finish an art program at a small community college. His difficulty completing classes at school is part of a lifelong pattern of procrastination and self-sabotage. When he was a child, his parents responded to his school anxieties by writing homework papers for him or calling the school with excuses. He grew up with a sense of "entitlement"—that the world would come to his rescue in much the same way his parents had. Unfortunately, this grew into a deep sense of self-doubt and low self-esteem when the world didn't always comply the way his parents had. In addition, the intense attentions of his mother led to an expectation that intimate relationships lead to smothering love. As a result, Karl has become pretty much of a loner.

Karl's Profile

	TRUST	AFFIRMATION	IDENTITY	COMPETENCE	INTIMACY	PURPOSE
55						
50						
45						
40						
35	■					
30	■					
25	■		■			
20	■	■	■			
15	■	■	■		■	
10	■	■	■		■	
5	■	■	■		■	■
0	■	■	■	■	■	■

What frustrates Karl the most in his life is that he is unable to bring his plans to completion. He procrastinates, but it is fear rather than laziness that causes this. Karl will benefit from the work in chapter 5, "When You Can't Achieve the Success You Desire," because it focuses on developing one's competence. He will benefit further from chapter 7, "When You Can't Find Meaning in Your Life." One of Karl's major dissatisfactions is that his life seems to have no purpose. Chapter 7 contains exercises and information that will help him develop a sense of direction and control.

Allison's Profile

Allison, thirty-six, is not a beauty and she knows it. It was pointed out countless times in her childhood. The fact that she was bright and vivacious wasn't enough for her family.

What she also knows is, she's terrific at math. As a child, math came easily to her, shocking those teachers who believed math wasn't something at which girls could excel. Her gift endeared her to her college roommates, though, because she could always be relied on for help with difficult math problems.

Her parents, however, never really understood her gift. This child who wanted a new calculator instead of pretty clothes was unlike her older sisters and a mystery to them. Her family always focused on her problems rather than her accomplishments.

Math still excites and motivates her after twenty years of working in the field. In addition, she has her marriage, her son, and a new house. She tells herself that she should feel satisfied. But what she has never seems enough and she's often vaguely depressed. She says, "I feel embarrassed to even admit this to anyone. Who am I to complain? What depresses me is that if you can work so hard, come so far, and still feel so—empty—what's the use?"

Allison's Profile

	TRUST	AFFIRMATION	IDENTITY	COMPETENCE	INTIMACY	PURPOSE
55						
50						
45						
40				■		
35				■	■	
30				■	■	■
25	■			■	■	■
20	■			■	■	■
15	■			■	■	■
10	■		■	■	■	■
5	■		■	■	■	■
0	■	■	■	■	■	■

People like Allison often feel guilty because outwardly they appear to have so much to be happy about. If they share their feelings of depression with other people, they are often told, "Don't be silly. Look at everything you have going for you." It is one of the most frustrating patterns a successful person can experience—to achieve so much, and not be able to feel happy about it. Chapter 3, "When Nothing Makes You Happy for Long," will help Allison explore the roots of this pattern and do the work necessary to begin to change it.

Charting Your Own Profile

Use the scores you obtained after you completed The Key Issues Inventory to complete your personal chart:

	TRUST	AFFIRMATION	IDENTITY	COMPETENCE	INTIMACY	PURPOSE
55						
50				51		
45						
		43				
40			39		38	40
35						
30						
	28					
25						
20						
15						
10						
5						
0						

Designing Your Treatment Plan

Your scores in each of the six areas will lead you to the chapters that will be of most value to you. Start with your lowest scores: they indicate the chapters you'll need to focus on most.

Key Issue	Chapter
Trust	Chapter 2 When You Can't Relax
Affirmation	Chapter 3 When Nothing Makes You Happy for Long
Identity	Chapter 4 When You Can't Stop Comparing Yourself to Other People
Competence	Chapter 5 When You Can't Achieve the Success You Desire
Intimacy	Chapter 6 When You Can't Find the Right Person
Purpose	Chapter 7 When You Can't Find Meaning in Your Life

Final Thoughts

You are embarking on a powerful journey of self-discovery. You will learn things about yourself that will open new doors to satisfaction and inner peace. You will also encounter "dark sides" that may bring up some shame and guilt and these feelings may discourage you. Be easy on yourself. It takes a lot of courage to confront old patterns. Furthermore, it takes a lot of perseverance to actually change old patterns.

It is an easy thing to decide you want to change your patterns, but it is a difficult thing to do. You may resist your own desire to change at times. This is to be expected. Just remember that your goal is one of greater happiness, satisfaction, and fulfillment. We can assure you that if you stay on course and complete the exercises in this workbook, you will learn to take more satisfaction in your pursuits and you will be on your way toward creating the life you truly desire.

> *Problems call forth our courage and our wisdom.*
> *It is because of problems that we grow mentally and spiritually.*
>
> —Scott Peck

Figure 1.2   The Six Keys to Creating the Life You Desire

2

When You Can't Relax

The First Key: Trust—Learning to Listen to Your Own Instincts and Rely on Others When It's Necessary

Understanding the Key Issue

Brittany and her best friend Diane were sampling tapas (Spanish appetizers), and struggling to hear each other above the noise. They were at a new restaurant packed with people who were seated so close, it seemed as though they were sitting at the same table with the two friends.

After listening to Brittany's plans for marketing a new account, Diane said, "It sounds like a great public relations campaign. You'll probably win an award, like last year."

"That was a fluke," Brittany replied, dismissing her past honor. "Two top agencies didn't get their entries in on time. Besides, I'll never get this done by the deadline. It's ten days away and I'm too swamped to put it together."

"Maybe they can give you more staff. After all, you're their top person."

Brittany shrugged. "They offered. I said, 'Forget it.'"

"Are you crazy? You know you can't do it all!"

Brittany sighed and moved her food around on her plate. She was too anxious to be hungry. She knew her friend wouldn't understand, but she tried to explain anyway. "They'd probably give me some entry-level person. I don't have time to train people."

"Did they say it would be an entry-level person?"

Brittany began to feel annoyed. She understands that her friend is trying to help, but she feels that no one really understands what she goes through. Ten years in this career, and every new campaign she creates still makes her feel as though she's auditioning for her job all over again. Why does she dig her heels in so hard when people tell her she should ask for some help? Why can't she just relax?

If Jon were in Brittany's place, he'd definitely ask for more assistants. He has had dozens of them in the past few years. He's trained college kids doing internships, entry-level people changing careers, and recent graduates recruited into his company when he's lectured on management at the local community college. He has a following of novices who love his sense of humor.

In the beginning, the assistants are thrilled to be assigned to him. But after the honeymoon period is over, the harder-working people grow to resent him. He won't let them *do* anything. They become frustrated straightening out files or crunching numbers. They feel like babies who aren't allowed to take their first steps and walk. When he does allow them to "walk," he hovers over them, and makes so many comments and corrections that any creativity they might have brought to the project is smothered by his overprotectiveness. They wonder, "Why can't he just relax?"

Sarah is finding that raising her daughter, Valerie, is the most anxiety-provoking job she's ever tackled. Valerie's pediatrician tries to do his best for her, but he has secretly labeled Sarah a "difficult" mom. Sarah's latest worry is, "I think Valerie is having sleeping problems. She complains that she wakes up a few times every night."

Six months ago, Sarah was worried that her daughter had low blood sugar. Even a five-hour glucose tolerance test, which was negative, didn't reassure her. Her doctor explains: "She's a pre-teen. It's a time of hormonal upheaval. Pre-teens come home from school and nap and then can't fall asleep later. Or they listen to loud music and watch TV all night and then they can't relax."

Sarah isn't reassured even though she knows the doctor's comments about the music and the TV are true. What she really thinks is, "He's placating me. We're HMO patients. If we weren't, I bet he'd do a full work-up on Val. Maybe she's anemic. I wish we could afford independent health insurance."

When you can't relax, even though a break from the turmoil of your troubled thoughts is exactly what you need and most desire, what could be the cause? Usually, the inability to relax is due to one or both of the following reasons:

- Hypervigilance. This is persistent anxiety that is fueled by heightened sensitivity to others; hypervigilance is often a result of a childhood in which there were too many adult responsibilities

- Compulsive Self-Reliance. This is the belief that you have to do it all by yourself to get it done right.

Let's look at these one at a time.

Hypervigilance: Do You Worry All of the Time?

One way to get high blood pressure is to go mountain climbing over molehills.

—Earl Wilson

There's an old joke about a psychiatrist who gently pointed out to a patient that most of the things he gets anxious about never actually happen. "I know," responds the patient nervously, "but then I worry about why they didn't happen."

Everyone experiences anxiety from time to time. But some of us live with that stressful, I-need-to-be-on-guard-every minute feeling constantly. Such people see scenarios of doom other people can't even imagine. For example, if as a child you were in a classroom and you heard your teacher say, "Some of you are not doing your homework diligently and it shows," you were convinced that the teacher was talking about you. Even though you had done your homework and had been diligent, you were sure you were being criticized. As an adult, if your boss waves you over at a party, you may think, "Oh no, what did I do wrong now?"

You've been told to relax and stop overdoing it so many times that you become angry and frustrated by your inability to change. But, deep down, you know that you're simply prepared for the worst and you think other people are naive if they don't do the same.

The chances are you're also a very sensitive person. You can walk into a room and instinctively know who is angry, who is depressed, and who needs to talk to you. Unfortunately, you tend to interpret much of what you see negatively.

It may be unconscious, but you live with a key belief that people are apt to let you down, not maliciously, but just as a matter of course. Therefore, you're anxious even when you are extremely well prepared. When you succeed, your success doesn't allay your fears. You still feel as though the axe could fall any moment.

If you identify with this description, take the following quiz to see how big a role anxiety plays in your life.

Measuring Your General Level of Anxiety

Questionnaire

Read each statement and put an X in the appropriate box (0 = never, 1 = rarely, 2 = occasionally, 3 = often, 4 = always).

	0	1	2	3	4
1. Do you find it difficult to stop worrying			X		
2. Do you have difficulty falling or staying asleep					X
3. Is muscle tension a frequent occurrence?				X	
4. Do you experience racing thoughts?					X
5. Do you fear something terrible is about to happen?			X		
6. Are you often plagued by fears of criticism?				X	
7. Do you experience racing or pounding heartbeats?		X			
8. Do you notice trembling or shakiness?		X			
9. Do you have frightening thoughts or nightmares?			X		
10. Are you afraid of losing control?			X		
11. Do you have difficulty concentrating?				X	
12. Do you feel tense or keyed up?				X	
13. Do you feel ready for something bad to happen?			X		
14. Do you have fears of imminent health problems or illness?			X		
15. Do you have trouble relaxing on vacations?			X		
16. Are you easily fatigued?		X			
17. Are you irritable?			X		
18. Does anxiety hamper your enjoyment of life?			X		
19. Do you have experiences of panic?			X		
20. Do you have worries about looking foolish?			X		

3   2L   7½   8
5   3,9
8

Your total score: _____ 47 _____

Scoring

0–20: You manage your stress very well. Although you experience anxiety at times, it probably passes quickly and doesn't interfere with your life.

20–40: Your anxiety level fluctuates from low to moderate. The exercises in this chapter will provide a good prevention strategy for keeping your stress levels down.

40–60: Your stress level is bordering on high. Now is the time to get to the root of what your anxious feelings are all about. The exercises in this chapter will help you to structure your life in a more balanced way.

60-80: Your anxiety level is very high. Apply the exercises in this chapter and consider talking about your anxiety with a medical specialist. You will benefit from committing to a consistent stress reduction program.

> *The time to relax is when you don't have time for it.*
>
> —Sydney J Harris

Anxiety: How Much Is Too Much?

Healthy Anxiety

All human beings experience fear. It is a universal emotion. On the physical level most people fear death, illness, injury, and hunger. On the psychological level we fear loss, abandonment, engulfment, or rejection. Anxiety is a milder form of fear.

One needn't try to completely extinguish fear. Anxiety and fear in their most natural forms exist to ensure survival. For instance, if you are walking across a street and hear the sound of a car horn, a jolt of fear may surge through your body, discharging a flow of adrenaline. This enables you to quickly jump out of harm's way. Or imagine a situation where you are watching TV when you should be studying for an important exam. It is very likely that you will feel a growing sense of anxiety. This feeling can serve as a wake-up call and get you back to your textbook and notes. These are examples of healthy anxiety.

Your goal is to learn how to manage anxiety so that it helps you when you need it as an impetus to action, but it doesn't inhibit you in situations where you should feel safe.

Chronic Anxiety

The *Diagnostic and Statistical Manual of Mental Disorders (DSM-IV)* is a highly regarded manual that mental health care professionals use when making a diagnosis from a patient's symptoms. One criterion of generalized anxiety disorder according to the *DSM-IV* is as follows:

> Excessive anxiety and worry (apprehensive expectation) occurring more days than not for at least six months, about a number of events or activities (such as work or school activities).

Other common symptoms of chronic or persistent anxiety include a rapid heartbeat, known as palpitations; irritability and edginess; upset stomach; sleep disturbances; fatigue; difficulty concentrating; headaches, muscle aches, backaches; and excessive worry.

Many people experience a level of anxiety that makes it difficult for them to concentrate or interferes with their ability to work or maintain relationships.

Causes of Chronic Anxiety

What causes people to develop persistent anxiety? Physical ailments, such as a thyroid disorder, are one possibility. Also, excessive caffeine or medications (antihistamines are the culprits in some cases) may be the cause.

You might even have a chemical imbalance. There is a growing body of evidence that persistent anxiety may be due to a chemical imbalance in the brain. This theory holds that people who suffer from anxiety have an excess of the neurotransmitter serotonin. Although there is no simple way to test the amount of serotonin one has, many people have found relief from chronic anxiety with medications that adjust their serotonin levels.

The most common reason for persistent anxiety, however, is an adaptation in childhood to constant stress. In other words, worry and hypervigilance (scanning the environment for indications that things may go wrong so that one can protect oneself) become habits that no longer require a trigger.

Jackie, a thirty-four-year-old legal assistant, recalls that even as a child she was always sure bad news was right around the corner. "No matter how hard I worked on a school project, I was always sure I was going to get a D or an F. I always did well, but I still had no self-confidence, no matter how often I got an A."

Jackie's history provides clues as to why she is always anxiously on guard, believing she's about to fail. "My grandparents lived through the depression, which made them compulsive about saving money. They'd deprived themselves of things like a TV or a more comfortable mattress. My parents were the same way. My father would go through the bills, shaking his head, and complaining that we were all spending too much money, and that he was on the verge of losing his job.

"My brother learned that my parents had more than a million dollars when he became executor of their estate. The 'poverty' I grew up in was all a big lie. But my father always felt poor. And I always feel scared about whether I'm saving enough, whether I'll lose my job, and whether I'll end up on the streets as a homeless person some day."

Donald, thirty-two, remembers his childhood this way: "My parents traveled a lot. They left us with a housekeeper who lived with us. She drank—usually from the moment they left until the day before they came home. One time she passed out on the kitchen table. I had no idea what to do; my parents were on a plane and my little sister was screaming at me to do something. But what could I have done? It was really scary."

There are many childhood experiences that can cause chronic anxiety and the feeling that one should never relax for a moment. Such experiences include the following:

1. Unpredictable home environments, such as those where a parent is battling an addiction like alcoholism, are very anxiety-provoking. Because it is impossible to predict what a drunk or stoned person is going to do, children in these environments learn to be on guard constantly.

2. Having a moderate or severe learning disability, or other physical, emotional, or intellectual challenge that interferes with school and learning, can be a cause of

constant anxiety. Being told that you're stupid or lazy when you're trying as hard as everyone else (or harder) can be frightening as well as frustrating.

3. A long-lasting childhood illness with all of the required tests, hospital stays, and strange symptoms can contribute to chronic anxiety.

4. The prolonged absence of a parent due to illness, death, or any other reason can contribute to the sense of chronic anxiety. If the absence happened suddenly, children may grow up with the feeling that just when they feel secure, the rug gets pulled out from under them.

5. A punitive school environment can promote anxiety. Regardless of how good a student you were, if you were yelled at and threatened in the classroom, that may have caused you to equate curiosity and the desire to explore with fear and verbal punishment.

This list could go on to include any number of experiences that make a child feel powerless and therefore anxious. It's also true that people can endure these situations without becoming chronically anxious adults. It's all in how we learn to cope. Some cope by withdrawing. They think, "I can't control this, so let's just forget about it and have a good time." They may grow into adults who never worry, even when they should. But the chances are good that if you can never relax, your way as a child was to seek control. It's wanting to have control in situations where we ultimately can't have it that causes much of chronic anxiety.

Some of us feel that to worry obsessively means we are doing something about a problem or that such worry will somehow "ward off evil." This is an illusion, but a comfortable one when you feel powerless over a situation.

A persistent sense of overresponsiblity is often the emotional overlay resulting from a challenging childhood in which the child felt responsible for keeping the peace or cleaning up other people's messes, emotional or otherwise. Such children can grow up with unwarranted guilt that comes from never being able to fix their families. Their belief that they should "be more" and "do more" permeates everything they do.

The key to changing the pattern begins with awareness. Do you really need to be on guard so much? Is your environment still threatening? Can you be prepared without being anxiously overprepared?

> *Workaholics anonymous probably has something to offer me,*
> *but I haven't had time to check it out yet.*
>
> —Mari

What's the Price You Pay for Never Being Able to Relax?

For your constant vigilance, you may get an illusion of control, the belief that you are protecting yourself from risk. These are no small benefits, but what is the cost? Here's a checklist of potential costs. Check the ones that apply to you.

	Never	Rarely	Sometimes	Often
Body Sensations				
Headaches		✓		
Stomachaches				✓
High blood pressure	✓			
Muscle tightness				✓
Emotions				
Anxiety			✓	
Depression			✓	
Suspicion			✓	
Guilt/Shame			✓	
Anger			✓	
Behaviors				
Overeating				✓
Alcohol consumption to relax you		✓		
Increased workaholic tendencies			✓	
Increased drug intake	✓			
Rescuing others			✓	
Thoughts				
Revenge fantasies		✓		
Feeling like a victim			✓	
Wanting to give up, run away			✓	
Persistent worries				✓

Relationship Tendencies				
Withdrawing			✓	
Caretaking			✓	
Withholding			✓	
Overresponsibility			✓	

Fear is that little darkroom where negatives are developed.

—Michael Pritchard

Exercise: Assessing the Costs

Take a look at your answers. Now write several sentences about the cost of never being able to relax.

The price I pay for being so anxious all the time is:

_____

_____

_____

_____

_____

_____

_____

_____

_____

Worry does not empty tomorrow of its sorrow;
it empties today of its strength.

—Corrie Ten Boom

Compulsive Self-Reliance: Do You Feel You're the Only One You Can Depend On?

Chronic anxiety often leads to what therapists call compulsive self-reliance. Think for a minute. How many people do you really depend on? How many times in the last twenty-four hours have you asked someone for help? How many responsibilities have you delegated to someone else in the last week? If your partner promises he'll water the garden, but he'll do it later, how confident are you that you won't have to remind him of his promise in the next three hours? How likely is it that the garden will no longer be on your mind, and that you won't keep checking to see if he does the job?

Compulsive self-reliance is a persistent sense of overresponsibilty. It is characterized by thoughts like these: "It's my fault that our division didn't get a bonus" and "It's my fault that mom's depressed."

It's compulsive in that we try to take control, even in situations where the responsibility isn't ours and shouldn't become ours. For example, you may be reluctant to hand over even your smallest burdens to others. You're part of a group, but you do all the work. You want your spouse to take a bigger role in parenting your children, but when he or she is away with the children without you, it makes you anxious. The fear isn't that the others might not survive without you. Unconsciously, you simply don't want to become dependent on anyone, or incur any form of emotional debt. You want to be the giver. The giver is always in control.

Kristen's Story

Kristen's story is a case in point. One summer her corporate office moved from the city to a new office building in the suburbs. Boxes of files and other materials she'd accumulated over five years stood in rows ten feet high in her new office. She unpacked and moved furniture until her back ached. Several times she hunted the halls for maintenance staff hired to help in the move. "They were always too busy," she recalls. "They were helping Rita down the hall, or Kara who is the type of person who breaks down and cries if someone moves her stapler. It was well past six when they came into my office and asked me if I needed anything. By then, I had everything already set up. I resented this eleventh hour appearance. Where were they when I needed them?"

Cheryl is a woman who knows Kristen well. She says this: "Kristen won't let people help her. She complains, but when you offer to do something for her, she always has a reason why she can't take you up on it. I'm not surprised that she had to unpack her whole office herself. Kristen always looks like she has it all together, and she generally does. You have to know her really well to understand how overwhelmed she gets with her own perfectionism. But she doesn't let most people see that."

Are You Compulsively Self-Reliant?

Self-reliance is a positive attribute. But do you have it to such a degree that it's causing chronic worry and disappointment in your life? The following quiz can help you determine whether you are overly self-reliant.

1. Imagine that you are a sixth-grade teacher. The principal introduces you to a young man who will be your student teacher for the rest of the term. It's a compliment that you've been chosen to train a new teacher. You look at the young man who will be in your classroom with you for the next two months and you think:

    a. "What a great chance to have a semester where I will never have to grade another spelling test." Visions of extra free periods when he will teach your class dance before your eyes.

    b. "I'll have to give him the class for three weeks. I better give him extensive lesson plans. Otherwise, these kids will do poorly on their standardized tests."

    c. "How can I get out of this? This throws a wrench in the successful progression of study it's taken me years to develop. I wouldn't mind an aide, but a student who takes over the class? Too much will be left to chance."

2. You and a friend plan to take an apartment together. She says she's found a marvelous rental agent. You want to know:

    a. Who to write the check to. You don't have free weekends to check out apartments and you trust a rental agent your friend adores to find you the best of the best.

    b. How to say, "Forget it," without alienating your friend. Rental agents are out to make money. You would rather see what's available yourself, even if you have to walk mountains of stairs and peer into other people's closets for a month.

    c. You would never use a rental agent. No one could possibly know what you really want.

3. You're at a management seminar. The instructor tells you that you will be divided into groups of four for an exercise on leadership. Your first thought is:

    a. "It's fun to work together and share ideas, rather than listen to a lecture. I like to hear what other people think."

    b. "I hate to work in groups. Why can't we just work alone?"

    c. "No way! What emergency can I think of to get out of here and back to the office where I can be productive?"

4. Your teenager is still failing algebra after the strong lecture you gave following her first poor report card. You are summoned to a meeting with her teacher and the department head. You think:

  a. "I want to learn exactly what she should be doing for homework each night, because she spends all night in front of the TV telling me she did it all during study hall. This meeting is going to help."

  b. "I'll have to tutor her every night and find some way to get her teachers to give her more time on tests."

  c. "She inherited this from me. I was never good at math and this is all my fault."

5. An ominous-looking notice from the IRS arrives in the mail. Your most likely response is:

  a. To hand it to your spouse and say, "You're the bookkeeper. How much more blood can they draw? You figure it out."

  b. To yell, "You wouldn't hire a professional to do our taxes, and now the IRS is on our backs." You insist that your spouse must examine every receipt and financial record.

  c. To cancel your life, as planned, for the next two weeks, so you can examine every piece of paper that supports your tax statement yourself. You knew you shouldn't have trusted anyone else to do your taxes.

6. You and your friends rent snowmobiles while on a vacation. When you set out on the trail, it begins to snow lightly. You think:

  a. "Great. This is an adventure. The snow is so pretty."

  b. "The snow is light so far, but what if it gets worse? Maybe we should go back. Half an hour will be plenty for me. Let's all go back for lunch."

  c. "Forget snowmobiling and let's turn back. I don't want to be in the woods on a questionable piece of machinery in the middle of a blizzard. Didn't anyone else see *Alive* or *Deliverance*?"

Scoring

Are most of your answers b's and c's? If so, you may suffer from compulsive self-reliance.

Control Versus Compulsive Self-Reliance

Self-reliance is a positive attribute. But compulsive self-reliance is *compulsive*. Don't confuse it with being a controlling person. You want control, but chances are good that you don't fit the classic definition of control freak. Consider the differences, as shown in the next table.

Controlling Person	Compulsively Self-Reliant Person
1. Wants everyone to do it his/her way.	1. Expects to be disappointed even if people do it his/her way, because no one else would give the same amount of time and effort.
2. Looks for people who can take over his/her responsibilities and be trained to do it his/her way.	2. Avoids delegating. Works around people.
3. Has little patience with other people's weaknesses or mistakes.	3. Accepts other people's faults but can't accept his/her own.
4. Asks questions and demands answers.	4. Figures it out with the help of books, articles, the Internet.
5. Takes control in a group.	5. Stays in the background, but is often the true leader in everything but name.
6. Gets angry when people make mistakes and lets them know it.	6. May blame others, but deeply believes the fault is still somehow ultimately his/hers.
7. When troubled by anxiety, buys self-help books, seeks treatment, complains if the treatment doesn't work immediately.	7. Has mixed emotions about seeking treatment for anxiety. "If I take a Xanax, I won't really be me. I should be able to calm myself down without chemicals.

Realizing Why It Will Never Be Enough

*It is an old ironic habit of human beings to
run faster when we have lost our way.*

—Rollo May

Chronic anxiety and the compulsive self-reliance it breeds can be a coping mechanism. The thought goes, "If I keep up my guard and if I worry enough, maybe I can ward off problems." But self-punishment is not a protection against trouble.

The goal—to be on top of future problems and be prepared for them—is an understandable one. But what is supposed to follow is the feeling that, finally, you have done enough, and you can then relax and feel happy. This rarely happens.

Diane, for example, suffered from both anxiety and compulsive self-reliance, especially when it came to being a parent. "I look at some of the pictures we took of the birthday parties we had for our twins with ponies, clowns, and magicians, and I think, 'What was this nonsense?'

"On weekends my husband would say, 'Why don't you just send them out to the yard to play? Or give them a coloring book if they're bored.' But I felt I had to provide them with all of these cultural experiences. We went to museums where they were bored, or plays where they couldn't sit still, and I blamed the play or the museum for not being

interesting enough. I thought of my own parents who had never encouraged my interest in art, so my kids had oil paints and art lessons when they were practically babies. I thought if I did an excellent job as a parent, I'd have excellent kids, and then I'd be able to relax.

"What do I have? One child who is too anxious to get off the couch, who can't pass his classes and depends on me for everything. The other is so rebellious she barely speaks to me. She says I embarrass her and that I'm too pushy. I thought I could relax when they grew up, but it's worse, not better."

Diane's experience isn't unusual. You might think that by taking on every responsibility and trying to achieve more and more, the day will come when you can finally relax. Too often that strategy backfires—and for understandable reasons:

You end up alone at the top. Such driven perseverance should be its own reward. But what happens is that you attract and even help to nurture or create procrastinators. Why should they do it, if they know you will, and you'll do it better?

Others may feel intimidated or invalidated by you. They may see you as aloof, detail-oriented or perfectionistic. They depend on you, but they also resent you for that and for having the kind of drive and work ethic they can't muster. Because you never seem to need it, no one gives you any help. Your reward for responsibility is more of the same, and that's why you never get a chance to relax.

You get people's grudging respect and even admiration. But because others don't see you as vulnerable, often they don't see you as lovable. It's vulnerability that causes other people to identify with us and to risk sharing themselves more fully to the point where they can risk a feeling of love. Admiration isn't the same as love, which is why so many admired people admit feeling lonely.

Your self-esteem becomes low. Who wouldn't have low self-esteem after trying to do it all and be it all, and still have to learn that your "all" isn't enough? You may have unconsciously set things up in your life so that you're your own sole source of validation. By this we mean that other people's praise or compliments go right over your head, as if they're meant for someone else. You rarely take praise in, or let it nourish you at the core. You think along these lines when you receive a compliment, "*Oh, he says nice things to everybody. . . . Anybody could have done this . . . I know the truth.*" What's true is that although anyone can do it, you're the one who actually does it.

The problem with relying on your achievements to fuel your self-esteem is that achievements are very short-lived. You may try six years to accomplish something, and then you get that award or that promotion. The satisfaction is very momentary when you think about it. An awards dinner, a promotion, a child's graduation, and the event is over in a flash.

What really builds self-esteem is the support and reassurance we receive along the way. If you can't absorb the reassurance, if you don't trust others who tell you how much they appreciate you, you end up feeling empty, even during those times when you reach what you thought would be the most fulfilling part of achieving your goals.

For these reasons, the key to overcoming your current frustration and dissatisfaction lies in dealing with the underlying issue of trust. Until you learn to trust, you can never really feel safe. Instead of focusing on more achievements or more protection from failure, you need to switch gears and begin to focus on gaining a sense of connection, on learning to ask for help and share responsibilities.

Rx: Building Trust and Learning to Relax

Your Key Questions

These key questions can help you stay focused on what the inner block is that is stopping you from feeling content or satisfied. Instead of focusing on the symptoms, they will help you to expand your thinking.

1. Am I often suspicious or mistrusting of people? How does this manifest itself in my life?
   (E.g., *I take on all responsibility myself; I keep a distance with others; I rarely let others know what I think or feel.*)

   _____

   _____

   _____

   _____

   _____

2. What lessons about trust did I learn in my childhood? How am I recreating the drama of my childhood?
   (E.g., *my family was always fighting or self-involved and it was impossible to count on anyone; I learned to rely only on myself; I learned people are not safe.*)

   _____

   _____

   _____

   _____

   _____

3. What price do I pay for never being able to relax or rely on others?
   (E.g., *I often feel overwhelmed, alone, stressed, and depressed.*)

   _____

   _____

   _____

   _____

4. If I felt people would consistently come through for me, how would my life be different?

(E.g., *I might ask for help more; I'd probably feel less isolated.*)

_____

_____

_____

_____

_____

See How Your Symptoms Serve You

You may have mixed emotions about giving up your anxieties and some of your self-reliance. On the surface worrying seems like a sensible mode. It feels as if you're taking some action that ultimately will be helpful.

We believe that many symptoms were once solutions that worked to fix or deal with past problems and trauma. Understanding how anxiety still seems to serve a protective purpose in your life is the first step in learning how to manage it

Example

Symptom	Protective Function
1. Hypervigilance (anxious scanning of the environment)	Attempt at creating safety in a dysfunctional family by constantly staying on guard.
2. Constant worry	An effort to continually solve problems, to protect oneself from harm. An illusion that you are taking action.
3. Compulsive self-reliance	Avoid being disappointed and hurt when others let you down. To feel in control.
4. Insomnia	Continued problem solving through the night. An illusion of always being ready to take action.
4. Anxiety through withheld anger	An attempt to protect others from our anger. To avoid conflict.
5. Avoiding closeness	Attempt to avoid possible hurt (as we may have experienced in the past).

Create New Choices

"I feel that if I don't push Mark every night to do his homework he'll never do it. The truth is with all my pushing he's still getting D's."

"I think my husband is cleaning-impaired. He'll vacuum if I harass him enough, but he vacuums around everything."

"I feel if I don't take over at meetings they'll go on forever. My boss has no backbone. In truth he's getting worse. I resent my boss so much it's ruining a career I'd otherwise enjoy."

Sound familiar? These are the words of clients who have realized there's a downside to this constant need to take control that goes beyond the anxiety it engenders. What about you?

Exercise: Finding New Solutions

- Write the symptoms you identified in "See How Your Symptoms Serve You" in the first column under "Symptom."

- Write the original protective function of this strategy in the second column under "Protective Function."

- Write the downside to this solution in the third column.

- Write a more effective solution to this problem in the fourth column.

Example

Symptom	Protective Function	Downside to This Solution	New Choices
Relying only on myself	Won't be let down or disappointed.	I end up stressed out. No one appreciates how much I do.	Learn who is trustworthy by observing them closely, communicate my needs clearly, learn to delegate and evaluate one day at a time.
Constant worry	Be prepared for anything	Can't relax	Select a specific time to focus on problems (i.e., 20 minute block at 3:00 PM Practice relaxation exercises

Now it's your turn.

Symptom	Protective Function	Downside to This Solution	New Choices
1.			
2.			
3.			
4.			

Your Vision of Change

How does one go about changing a lifetime pattern? For most of us, it begins with a vision. Take a deep breath. Exhale fully and completely. Now, imagine your life relatively free of anxiety and mistrust. (You don't have to believe this completely yet. Developing the skill of active imagination means acting "as if" your thoughts are true.)

See yourself as capable of enlisting others for support and trust. Imagine what your life would feel like if you were to balance work with play. What activities would you participate in to help minimize your stress levels? How would your life be different?

Take a deep breath and see yourself this way as if it were your current reality. Notice any resistance you may feel and just let it gently drift away.

Karen's Vision

I see myself reacting less to others and believing more in myself. I am more resilient. I go with the flow more easily.

I see myself developing a circle of friends who I can trust. I take small risks to see if people are indeed safe for me to rely on. I find that some of them are.

I see myself letting my children take some of the consequences of their actions and I trust that they are strong enough to cope with frustration. I see myself not bringing the lunch they left at home to the school. I see myself at work saying "No" to being on another committee. I take time each day to do something pleasurable. In these moments I actively choose to let go of my worries and concerns. I see myself balancing work and play. I feel happy.

Now, write out your personal vision.

_____

_____

_____

_____

_____

_____

_____

_____

_____

Determine Who You Can Trust

Trust in yourself. Your perceptions are often more
accurate than you are willing to believe.

—Claudia Black

We could tell you that you'd relax more if you trusted other people to come through for you. Chances are you'd agree. But let's consider whether or not you have a basis for your lack of trust. If you have good reasons not to trust, no amount of coaching you to trust is going to help.

What Do You Really Need?

The following quiz identifies the five most trust-enhancing qualities in a relationship. Think about a primary relationship in your life and answer the following questions.

Read each statement and mark X in the appropriate box (0 = never, 1 = rarely, 2 = moderately, 3 = often, 4 = always).

	0	1	2	3	4
1. **Empathy.** Do you feel listened to and understood				X	
2. **Acceptance.** Do you feel accepted, without judgment, for who you truly are				y	

3. **Consistency.** Is there a sense of predictability in your interactions?			X	
4. **Safety.** Do you feel it is safe to express yourself without retribution? Are you physically safe?		X		
5. **Honesty.** Do you feel this person is straightforward and honest with you?			X	

12

Scoring

0–5: You receive almost no building blocks for trust. Take a good hard look at the reasons you continue with this relationship.

6–9: This relationship is very skimpy on trust and support. Be more assertive with your needs or reconsider your choices.

10–14: You have a good foundation for trust, but you still need to work on expressing your needs and expanding intimacy.

15–20: This is a solid base of support, which is a strong foundation for trust.

Your Circle of Safety

*The hardest thing to learn in life is which
bridge to cross and which to burn.*

—Laurence J. Peter

As you progress along your journey toward personal growth, you will notice an interesting phenomenon: not all of your friends and family will like or appreciate your change. Some people may even try (directly or indirectly) to encourage you to return to your old ways. Expect this. If your score in the last exercise was low, you need to choose your personal growth support team carefully.

During the process of rebuilding trust, the key challenge lies in determining who is safe and who is not. If you grew up in a family where trust was often violated, this is often difficult for you to determine.

One way is to notice how people you are inclined to trust interact with you and others. Do you find they gossip critically about others? *"Your Uncle Joe is a lazy bum."* Do they make commitments they do not keep? *"Okay, I said six o'clock but I can't help it if I'm forty minutes late."* Do they betray confidences? *"I didn't think you'd mind me telling Mom about your problems with your husband."*

Trust your eyes, ears, and intuition. Mistrustful people leave a lot of writing on the wall. But it's up to you to read it.

Exercise: Your Circle of Safety

Next, you will see a circle. Write the names of a few people who seem to be consistently honest and trustworthy within the circle. Write the names of those who have betrayed you or displayed a lack of trust with others outside of the circle.

Your Circle of Safety

"Safe" people and reasons why they are safe:

1. _____

2. _____

3. _____

Unsafe people and reasons why they are not safe:

1. _____

2. _____

3. _____

One person who I feel it might be safe to begin to trust more this week is:

_____

Building Trust: Weeding Your Own Garden

Many of our clients are constantly looking for moments they believe to be inevitable when they will be let down or betrayed by others. Yet they focus so exclusively on others that they fail to see their own lapses in trust.

For example, Joyce, a thirty-four-year-old accountant, came into therapy complaining about the countless times men had betrayed her. She wondered whether she could ever learn to trust a man. But a curious pattern emerged in her first few months of therapy. She came late to sessions consistently and missed other sessions without calling. At times it would take her days to even return our calls. When she did call back, her excuses would be something like "I got so busy I couldn't get to a phone." We began to wonder, *Can we trust her?*

What soon became apparent was that Joyce had a long-standing pattern of "stretching the truth." While she viewed this as harmless, it was obvious that the very thing she craved in others, trustworthiness, was precisely what she was unable to practice herself.

When we are dishonest ourselves, and disown our own dishonesty, invariably we project it onto others. If we want to see others as worthy of our trust, it is critical that we must first practice what we preach—we must become trustworthy people ourselves.

Exercise: Taking Your Own Integrity Inventory

The notion that we're not completely honest or honorable in everything we do can be hard to acknowledge. But who among us is always completely truthful? Sometimes we believe that if we are straightforward about our behavior, we will harm ourselves. We're only human. We are driven to protect ourselves.

Make a list of the ways you are not completely honest with others. Do you show up for your appointments on time? Do you inflate or deflate your successes? Can people count on you to do what you say? Do you always tell people what you really think or feel?

1. _____

2. _____

3. _____

4. _____

5. _____

As difficult as this assignment may seem to be, if you do it in good faith, it will help you to recognize that if we are constantly attempting to cover our tracks, we are also constantly refueling our anxieties.

Jack, forty-six, admitted, "I'll tell you the truth, the reason I finally stopped lying once and for all was because it was exhausting making up one falsehood after another. Near the end, I could hardly keep my own stories straight. In therapy I learned that half the things I was trying to hide from others didn't matter to anyone anyway. Now I feel so much more relaxed. What you see is what you get."

Combating Compulsive Self-Reliance

Exercise: Asking for Help

Do you want to make some headway on tackling your underlying issue of trust so that you can finally learn to relax? This next assignment requires you to ask five different people for help.

If you identify with the concept of being compulsively self-reliant, this may be one of the most difficult things you will ever do. Remember trust is only built through experience. You need to create new experiences. *Choose people who are most likely to come through for you!* Remember if you want to validate your belief that people are not to be trusted, you can choose people who are guaranteed to let you down (you know who they are).

Here are some possibilities:

Ask for directions. Ask for a recipe. Ask a friend, "How do you handle it when your child whines?" Ask your spouse for help with the dishes. Ask for a back rub. Ask for an answer to a question for which you already know the answer.

List five times you can ask for help over the next week, even when you don't really need it. **Example:** "I'll ask Joe what mutual fund he invests in."

1. _____

2. _____

3. _____

4. _____

5. _____

Exercise: Learning to Delegate Responsibility

Make a list of every responsibility you took on today. Next to it write who you could have delegated it to. Have fun with this one. Here's a chance to take a close look at all you do. You might even choose to write about a day when you were not at work. Here, for example, is a list one of our clients generated about a day off from work—when she was supposed to be relaxing.

1. Watered plants, weeded garden

2. Paid bills

3. Fed cats

4. Made bed

5. Mailed bills

6. Called for dinner reservations

7. Changed cat litter

8. Picked up dry cleaning

9. Prepared and cooked dinner

10. Cleaned out refrigerator

11. Did laundry

12. Returned daughter's library books

13. Drove kids to baseball practice

Letting Go of Control

Were you able to find enough people to delegate responsibilities to in the last exercise? Letting go isn't easy. Let's take a look at what letting go is really all about—why it's crucial.

What Letting Go Means

- That we cannot control the thoughts, behaviors, or feelings of other people. Other people do things their own way and situations have their own outcomes, in spite of our efforts at controlling behavior or outcomes.

- It means to stop rescuing others from the consequences of their own behavior, so that they can learn and grow.

- It means that no matter how much control we have over a situation, the results are never quite what we planned.

- It means that we need to focus on what we need to change in ourselves rather than arguing and obsessing about others' shortcomings.

- It means that we have limitations, and that attempts to hide our limitations cause many problems in our lives.

- It means that you cannot change others; you can only change yourself.

What Letting Go Does Not Mean

- That you will stop caring about others.

- That you have failed.

- That something terrible will happen.

- That you must cut yourself off completely from others.

Exercise: What's the Worst Thing That Could Happen?

"If I let go of my attempt to control, it's going to mean disaster." We know exactly what you are feeling because we've been there, too. But we're going to try to persuade

you to take a chance anyway. You can always go back to compulsive self-reliance and the tension of needing to control everything. The key question is, could you be just a little wrong about the people in your life? Would they come through for you if you gave them the chance? Don't you want to know?

To-Do List for Letting Go

1. Pick three specific areas in your life in which you would like to stop being so controlling. Phrase them as goals.

2. Next answer the question, "What's the worst thing that could happen," if you don't meet your goals?

Examples

1. The Goal: I will ask my husband to clean the kitchen and empty the garbage.
   The worst that could happen: a dirty kitchen and smelly garbage.

2. I will let my assistant do half of our next presentation.
   The worst that could happen: He might get long-winded and bore people, we could lose the account.

3. I could let my son do his next book report without almost doing it for him.
   The worst that could happen: The teacher would say it's not good enough and why.

Now look at your own To-Do list. Choose one goal to risk letting go of control this week.

Time-Limited Worry

People with a generalized anxiety condition worry around the clock. This worry has no boundaries and tends to be unproductive. This exercise instructs you to find a *specific time of the day* to worry and obsess about your problems in order to free up the rest of the day. When you know that you have set aside a part of the day to do nothing but worry about specific issues, this can help you to let go of "generalized" nonspecific worrying during the rest of the day.

For example, if you spend a lot of time worrying about money throughout the day, plan to focus on your financial concerns during a specific period of time (i.e., from 6:00–6:45 PM) on a daily basis. Start a special journal designed just for your worries. During the period of time you allot to worrying, write about all your concerns and possible solutions in this special journal.

Example: Jeff's Journal Entry

There's never enough money . . . I'm so angry at how easy other people have it . . . I'm always trying to make ends meet . . . How will I plan for my retirement? . . . My wife spends too much money . . . It's so frustrating . . . If only I could win the lottery . . . How can I make more money? . . . Maybe I can learn about investments . . . Yes . . . I should sign up for an adult education course in managing money . . . I can find one tomorrow . . . That feels better . . . I'll do that tomorrow.

Example: Sally's Journal Entry

I'll never find a husband . . . All the good men are taken . . . It's too late for me, I'm thirty-seven . . . I'm not pretty enough . . . Men only want younger women . . . It makes me so angry . . . All my past relationships have failed miserably . . . It's so depressing . . . Why is it easier for other women? . . . Boy do I sound like a victim . . . but at least it feels good to express my feelings . . .

Many people discover that if they give themselves active permission to worry or complain for a set amount of time, it helps create an internal shift in their emotions from victim-oriented thinking to solution thinking. Try it for yourself.

Exercise: The Serenity Prayer

When we can't relax due to fear and mistrust, we compulsively hold on to control. This "solution" unfortunately only leads to more fear and anxiety. The Serenity Prayer exercise is a powerful exercise for letting go of control. The Serenity Prayer, a staple of twelve-step programs, goes like this:

"God, grant me the serenity to accept the things I cannot change,

The courage to change the things I can, and the wisdom to know the difference."

How can you use this prayer to help you let go of trying to control others' behavior or the outcome of your own behavior? Perhaps hearing how others have used it will help you to understand the concept more easily.

Jan, forty-five, has been in an abusive relationship with her husband, Joe, for nearly twenty years. Her role in her family of origin was much the same. She grew up with an abusive father. Her "solution" had always been to try to make peace. Yet this strategy never seemed to change any of the repeating patterns of abuse and neglect.

With the help of individual therapy and a support group it finally became clear that "hoping" her husband would change was not enough. She needed to strengthen her personal power and take a stand to meet her own needs. She also needed to use her support system to help validate her new stronger identity.

She used the Serenity Prayer in the following way to help her understand what behavior she needed to change and what behavior she was willing to accept without attempting to change it.

God grant me the serenity to accept the things I cannot change . . .

I can't change my husband's abusive treatment of me.

the courage to change the things I can . . .

I can tell him clearly that if he continues this behavior I will leave.

and the wisdom to know the difference.

I can recognize that I might not be able to change my husband, but I can change my reaction to him. I can stop making excuses and concentrate on my own assertiveness issues and on building a support group for myself. That will help me to make the decision to leave or stay with greater clarity.

Now it's your turn.

1. God grant me the serenity to accept the things I cannot change . . .

_____

_____

_____

the courage to change the things I can . . .

_____

_____

_____

and the wisdom to know the difference.

_____

_____

_____

2. God grant me the serenity to accept the things I cannot change . . .

_____

_____

_____

the courage to change the things I can . . .

_____

_____

_____

and the wisdom to know the difference.

_____

_____

_____

Stress Management Can Be Fun

Tension is a habit. Relaxing is a habit.
Bad habits can be broken, good habits formed.

—William James

Tackling some of the issues underlying your inability to relax is just one step. The next step is to learn new techniques to manage your anxiety and stress. The following exercise is designed to spark your creativity with stress management. Read the following list of simple stress reduction ideas. Then choose your favorites or make up your own.

Simple Pleasures for Relaxation

1. Take a walk in the woods

2. Rent a comedy video

3. Listen to a side of a favorite album

4. Take a snooze

5. Stretch to music

6. Pet a cat or dog

7. Build a model

8. Sculpt clay into a figure no one can recognize

9. Listen to a meditation tape

10. Exercise while watching a video

11. Buy some fresh flowers and arrange them in a beautiful vase

12. Cook some homemade soup

Now write down a list of your top five favorite pleasures. (Feel free to use your own ideas.)

1. _____

2. _____

3. _____

4. _____

5. _____

When you have completed your list of your five favorite pleasures for relaxing, write the following sentence at the bottom of the list and sign your name to it. Then, use a magnet to attach the page to your refrigerator, so that you will be sure to see it several times a day.

I commit to doing at least one fun stress management activity every day this week.

(Your signature) _____

The Power of the Present for Relaxing

Most of our anxieties focus on fears of the future or concerns over the past. We ruminate in our minds searching for answers, but we usually only end up feeling even more agitated. Living within a mindset of compulsive worry only creates more of the same.

A powerful exercise for breaking this chronic worry cycle is to center yourself in the present moment. Whenever you feel out of control with your worry, repeat the following phrase:

At this moment . . . and then finish the sentence

Example

- At this moment . . . I am taking a deep breath.

- At this moment . . . I see the blue sky.

- At this moment . . . I am hearing the sounds of the ocean on a tape.

- At this moment . . . I am typing at the computer.

- At this moment . . . I am stretching my neck.

- At this moment . . . I am petting my cat.

- At this moment . . . I am aware I am slouching and I straighten up.

- At this moment . . . I am feeling grateful for my health.

- At this moment . . . I am taking another deep breath.

- At this moment . . . I am smelling the salt air.

- At this moment . . . I am tasting the sweetness of an orange.

It will be helpful to focus your awareness on your five senses: sight, hearing, touch, smell, and taste. As simple as this exercise is, it is an extremely powerful stress reducer. It will also get you in touch with your body and out of the worry cycle.

Meditation and Guided Imagery

To be idle requires a strong sense of personal identity.

—Robert Louis Stevenson

One of the most powerful ways to achieve a consistent ability to relax is through the practice of *deep relaxation*. There are many techniques that can lead you to the state of being deeply relaxed, including meditation, hypnotherapy, and guided imagery work. The bottom line is essentially the same for the various disciplines—deep relaxation of our minds and bodies isn't something that just happens, it is something we can create.

The daily practice of twenty minutes of deep relaxation will produce the following results: 1) a more generalized sense of relaxation each day; 2) increased energy and production levels; 3) more restful sleep at night; 4) a reduction of psychosomatic illnesses.

Exercise: Relaxation with a Guided Meditation

Here is a relaxation exercise that many of our clients have found helpful:

Find a comfortable place where the are no distractions. Take the phone off the hook or tell your family not to disturb you for a half hour. If possible, put on some soothing peaceful music. Have someone read the following script to you or record it into a tape recorder for playback.

Script

Go to a quiet place and realize that for the next few minutes there is nothing you need to do and nothing you need to figure out. . . . It's a time to gently relax. . . . Begin by taking in a nice deep breath . . . You may imagine yourself breathing in relaxation and breathing out tension. . . . Feel the coolness of the air through your nose. . . . With each breath feel a wave of relaxation come through your body. . . .

Imagine yourself at the top of a beautiful staircase with ten steps. . . . Design this staircase anyway you like. . . . As you slowly walk down the steps you feel calmer and more relaxed. . . . As you go deeper and deeper into a wonderful state of relaxation . . . you begin to feel calmer and calmer. . . . Your body feels heavier as your muscles let go and begin to feel limp and relaxed. . . . Imagine a golden light passing through your body and filling you with a sense of peace and contentment . . . When you arrive at the bottom of the staircase, you open a door to the most scenic spot you can imagine. . . . Feel the breeze. . . . Smell the air and flowers. . . . Use all your senses to see, hear, smell, feel, and touch the beauty of this place. . . . Absorb yourself in the splendor and relaxation of this scenic spot. . . .

Now see yourself just as you'd love to be. . . . Notice how healthy you look. . . . Feel how your muscles are strong and resilient. . . . Take a deep breath. . . . You are relaxed. . . . In your mind's eye you see your life exactly as you wish it would be. . . . Everything is easy. . . . Everything works out and makes sense in a way you never imagined before. . . . You can relax because you know that you don't need to do anything right now. . . . You don't have to be anything. . . . You are enough exactly as you are. . . . This moment will strengthen you. . . . You are nourishing yourself . . .

*You are getting stronger as you relax and let go. . . . Now spend a few minutes in
this scenic spot doing whatever feels relaxing and nurturing. . . . Take your time. . . .
Enjoy yourself. . . .*

*When you feel ready, at the count of five, gently come back to the room. . . .
One, gently start to stretch. . . . Two, take a breath as you start to awaken. . . .
Three, open your eyes. . . . Four, feel awake, alive, and refreshed . . . and Five, feel
ready to continue your day with renewed energy!*

You will find that each time you go into a state of deep relaxation, it will become easier to access. The more you practice, the easier it becomes.

Now, more than ever, there is an increasing selection of cassette tapes and compact discs with guided imagery experiences available for you to buy. Look in your local bookstore or check out Amazon.com for a variety of selections. The audiotape, "A Path to Serenity—A Guided Meditation" by Mitch Meyerson, is available directly from the author. See the back page of this book. There is also a list of audiotapes and compact discs in the back of this book in the section called "Resources" that will help you choose what you need.

Music for Relaxation and Imagination

> *Music has the capacity to touch the innermost reaches of
> the soul and music gives flight to the imagination.*
>
> —Plato

Many of us are so caught up in the hectic pace of life that we barely have time to stop for lunch. And, when we do take a lunch break, it is often with our next project propped up on the table in front of us. We desperately need time to slow down.

One wonderful way to relax is to bracket off ten to fifteen minutes, close the door, turn on the answering machine for the phone, dim the lights, and turn on the stereo or put on a pair of headphones. Find a CD or cassette of your most relaxing or enjoyable music and listen just for the pleasure of it.

In just a short time, you will find that your mood will change and your muscles will begin to relax. Take a few of deep breaths. You will be amazed at the results. The hardest part of doing this is deciding to take the time. The next exercise is just for fun. Make a list of your ten favorite records of all time. Maybe this list will inspire you to drag out some old LPs from your closet and listen to them again.

My Ten Favorite Records of All Time!

1. _____

2. _____

3. _____

4. _____

5. _____

6. _____

7. _____

8. _____

9. _____

10. _____

New Thoughts and New Actions

Men are not prisoners of fate, but only prisoners of their own mind.

—Franklin D. Roosevelt

Positive Affirmations to Say to Yourself

- Relaxing is a habit that I will practice today by beginning with a deep breath and a stretch.

- Today, I will build trust by learning to listen to and trust my own intuitive voice.

- It's okay to relax and enjoy myself.

- Colleagues can be resources, not just competition.

- Every day I am learning to balance work and play.

- Today, I will ask for what I want and need.

- I am willing to accept those things I cannot control.

- It's okay to delegate tasks to others.

- I will take time today to play.

- I can choose to be a member of a group, not always the exception.

- With every breath I take, I breathe in relaxation and breathe out tension.

- My feelings are as valuable as my accomplishments.

- The past is no longer; the future has yet to arrive. The only moment that is real is right now.

Positive Things You Can Do for Yourself

- Schedule time each day for slowing down, resting, stretching, or napping to avoid stress-related problems. Exercise and/or massage are also great stress reducers.

- From time to time, ask for help. Although this is difficult for you, it will help you build trust in others and create more time for yourself. Start simple: ask someone to scratch your back the next time it itches.

- Share your feelings with close friends or a therapist. Expressing your anger, hurt, sadness, or depression will lower your stress level, minimize psychosomatic illnesses, and help you build intimate relationships with others.

- Schedule a vacation and leave your obligations at home.

- Delegate simple tasks to others. Have your husband do the dishes, have your laundry delivered by a service, have your secretary type your correspondence, and have your son mow the lawn.

- Spend time in the garden, go to a ballgame, create an adventure to break the routine (drive home through a new neighborhood).

- Learn to say "No."

- Make a list of all the enjoyable things you'd like to do but haven't had time, and commit to doing one this week.

- Take a class on stress management. Join a yoga group. Play tennis, golf, or any physical activity that brings you pleasure.

- Learn to forgive yourself and others for shortcomings and mistakes.

3

When Nothing Makes You Happy for Long

*The Second Key: Affirmation—
Learning to Recognize Your Feelings
and Accomplishments and Affirm
Their True Value*

Understanding the Key Issue

Ellen, twenty-seven, began designing jewelry in college. Ten years later she had her own small company, loyal customers, and moderate success. "I knew if I could just get my line of jewelry into department stores, it would take my business to a new level," she recalls. "The drudgery of art fairs, dragging tables and shelves, and feeling like the Swamp Thing in the heat, would be over.

"I pitched dozens of stores. Then it happened. A new buyer for a major chain took half of my line of earrings and most of the bracelets. The order was huge. But the jewelry was barely packed and shipped when I began thinking, *Why didn't she order any necklaces?*

Why doesn't she like them? And the picture frames. She barely looked at them. The necklaces and frames were the newest part of my line. I'd had such hopes for them and they were going nowhere." My husband threw up his hands. "You know something?" he said, "You're never satisfied. Nothing makes you happy."

Michael, forty-six, can identify with Ellen. "I've spent thousands of dollars on health club memberships, vacations, new cars, tennis lessons, you name it. I was into tropical fish for a time and had to have every exotic fish that ever lived in my fish tank. Then I got into tai chi. I became so engrossed in tai chi most of my fish died. I always think, *This is going to be it. This is what is what is going to make me feel content.* It never is."

Susie, thirty-four, is also frustrated. "I'd dated a slew of men. I was tired of that same old conversation: 'What do you do? Oh, how interesting.' Watching videos with my cat was starting to be more exciting. But it's like they say. When you aren't looking, you find it and that's how it was with Ron. He told me he loved me. Every time he said it I thought, 'Something is going to come along and ruin this. It isn't going to work out.'

"Every kiss, every evening together, this is what I thought until I realized something. He wasn't the one making me feel this way. Something inside *me* wouldn't allow me to be happy for long."

If the preceding stories sound familiar, you aren't alone. You may find that worry, frustration, and negativity are frequent companions. Other people point out all the reasons why you should feel grateful for what you have. Why do you seem to throw happiness away with both hands?

There's actually a term for this state of mind: *anhedonia*. It means the absence of joy. Anhedonia was derived from the Greek *an*, meaning "not," and *hedone*, meaning —"pleasure," thus anhedonia means the inability to experience pleasure. (The original title for Woody Allen's film *Annie Hall* was *Anne Hedonia*.) Furthermore, as strange as it may sound, this anhedonia actually serves a purpose in your life. In the sections that follow we will look at the most important reasons why many people find it difficult to stay happy for long, and what you can do to dramatically change the "never enough" pattern.

Most self-defeating patterns were originally *solutions* to earlier life problems. (e.g., if you were slapped every time you got angry, the obvious "solution" would be to deny or repress that emotion). In essence, we learn to adapt to our circumstances in order to create safety for ourselves. Unfortunately, these solutions become ingrained as a way of being and we don't realize that we have choices about such matters.

In the following sections you will create a wider range of options and choices for yourself. By doing so you will create the conditions to feel greater satisfaction in your life. Let's begin with the following questionnaire which will help you determine your capacity for experiencing and maintaining happiness.

Measuring Your General Level of Anhedonia

Questionnaire

Read each statement and put an X in the appropriate box (0 = never, 1 = rarely, 2 = moderate, 3 = often 4 = always).

	0	1	2	3	4
1. Do you find moments of happiness rare or short-lived?			X		
2. When you think about your hopes and dreams, do you start to feel tired or overwhelmed?			X		
3. Are you very self-critical?				X	
4. Do people tell you that you tend see the negative in most situations?				X	
5. Do you have poor concentration or difficulty making decisions?			X		
6. Do you feel sad or blue most of the time?			X		
7. Do you lack energy?			X		
8. Do you feel empty right after you've achieved one of your goals?			X		
9. When something good happens, do you think it's the calm before the storm?			X		
10. Do you find it hard to motivate yourself to do things?			X		
11. When you talk to your family, does the conversation seem to gravitate toward problems?				X	
12. Do you feel vaguely unhappy without any real reason for unhappiness?				X	
13. Is it hard to find anything you're really interested in?				X	
14. Does your future seem gloomy?			X		
15. Do you think that life is not worth living?				X	
16. Are you sleeping too much, or having trouble falling asleep at all?				X	
17. Do you have little interest in sex?				X	
18. Do you often find yourself complaining about your life?				X	
19. Do you feel inferior to others?				X	
20. Do you have trouble accepting compliments?				X	

Your total score: _____50_____

Scoring

25 points or less: You may have had a recent blow to your self-esteem or frustrations with your job or a relationship. But you weather these storms well. When the storms pass, you revert to a pattern of optimism and general satisfaction. The unhappiness you feel now will most probably pass, and you will begin to feel more like yourself again soon.

26–35 points: You tend to worry, and to ruminate at times about your future. You don't take happiness for granted, but you don't throw it away with both hands either. The exercises in this chapter will help you to clarify your goals so that you can direct your energies where you will gain the most happiness.

36–50 points: You don't consider yourself a pessimist, but a realist. You obsess about what could go wrong in any situation. You have experienced a lot of success, but your problem is that you don't take the time to reap your rewards or to enjoy them. You're too busy saying, "Yeah, but . . ." The exercises in this chapter will help you rid yourself of the obstructions that prevent you from enjoying peace of mind. You've earned it—or you have the capability to earn it. You need to get out of your own way.

50 or more points: You are unhappy, in spite of your achievements, your relationships, your life. Worry and frustration are such a part of your life that you wonder if it's a genetic personality problem—something you were born with. It's not. It's a pattern that made excellent sense at one point in your life and that you can begin to let go of today.

Discovering the Roots of Your Struggle

What are some of the root causes of anhedonia or dysthymia? Sometimes there is no clear cause. But for many people it's an outgrowth of the following:

1. A depressive retreat from feelings cuts you off from your connection with your own emotions—both good and bad.

2. A problem-focused family that taught you to dwell on the negative aspects of life more than the positive, which has led you to concentrate on problem-focused thinking to the exclusion of other kinds of thoughts.

3. A chemical imbalance that exacerbates your tendency to look on the dark side.

4. A way of perceiving and relating to the world that actually creates more suffering for you.

Now let's look at these issues one at a time.

The Depressive Retreat from Feelings

There's an old joke: Two elderly women are at a Catskill Mountain resort and one of them says, "Boy, the food is really terrible." The other one says, "Yeah I know, and such small portions." Well, that's essentially how I feel about life.

—Woody Allen (opening lines
to *Annie Hall*)

If you can never stay happy for long, an obvious question is, do you suffer from chronic low-grade depression? Michael, thirty-three, described it this way: "I can't point to anything in my life that is making me feel depressed. It's just a lingering type of unhappiness that hangs on. It seems like I've always felt this way." This type of depression is known as *dysthymia*. Along with the blues, people who suffer from dysthymia often have some kind of eating disorder, trouble concentrating, sleep disorders, and often attempt to lift their moods through alcohol or other illegal substances.

Although people who have dysthymia usually do not have the hopeless sense of despair commonly seen in clinical depression, they have a great deal of difficulty sustaining any feeling of pleasure. As one man put it, "I just feel flat."

Dysthymia sometimes develops when a person cannot cope with his or her feelings. The person filled with anger or pain that has become unbearable retreats not just from the troublesome feelings, but from all feelings in general. It is a protective way of restoring some sense of control over life.

Michael Franz Basch explained this in *Understanding Psychotherapy* (1988),

Depression indicates that the self system has had to retreat to a lower level of functioning in the face of its inability to meet higher goals. Depression also serves as a communication, a message to the world at large that the self system can no longer be counted upon, that it has ceased to function in some significant degree, that one has lost hope, and that help must come from the outside.

Could your present unhappiness be a depressive retreat from feelings? Take the following short quiz and find out. Place a check mark next to the statements that are true for you.

Questionnaire

1. I intellectualize my relationships, analyzing what he or she said rather than what I feel.	✓
2. I cry when I am really angry.	✓
3. I tend to withdraw from people who are too emotional.	✓
4. I can be the picture of strength when I feel that I am crumbling inside.	✓

5. I think that if I expressed my feelings, they would become too big and unmanageable. I would lose control.	
6. I turn to substances (alcohol, drugs, or food) or to work to avoid feeling depressed or anxious.	
7. I believe that emotions are a sign of weakness. (Men shouldn't cry, women shouldn't get angry.)	
8. I feel emotionally flat much of the time.	

Be gentle with yourself as you reflect upon your answers. Everyone has a unique style of managing their emotions. These management techniques are usually adaptive responses to our childhood environments. Look at your answers as helpful feedback.

A Problem-Focused Family Creates a Problem-Focused Child

My grandfather used to make home movies and edit out the joy.

—Richard Lewis

In some families, the only conversation that exists between the parents and children is focused on problems. As one woman put it, "If I didn't talk to my mother about my diet and how much trouble I have losing weight, I can't imagine what we'd talk about."

Sometimes we feel our parents love us the most when we're in trouble, because that's when we get their attention. "My parents practically threw money at me when I was messing up," says Ryan, twenty-seven. "Now that I'm doing better, they won't even send me an airline ticket to visit them. They're too busy supporting my brother who is the one who is messing up now. In my family, you are rewarded for failure."

The lesson seems to be "When you're troubled and depressed, people care more." It becomes a whole style of relating to the people we are close to. Voicing fears and insecurities is our way of bonding with others. When you study problem-focused families closely, one thing becomes obvious. People talk about their problems, obsess about them, advise each other, but there is very little action. Someone growing up in such a family begins to believe that worrying and feeling depressed is actually doing something to overcome the problems. Such a history leads to "there is never-enough" mindsets.

Exercise: Are You a Problem-Focused Thinker?

From the following list, select the answer that sounds most like you.

1. A close friend reads your new short story and says it's wonderful and should be published. You think:

a. She's pulling my chain. She probably didn't read the whole thing.

b. What does she know anyway? She's not a writer.

c. This is great! I knew it was a good story and it's nice to get a compliment.

2. You have a great financial week at work. Your boss is giving you a bonus. You think:

a. Something bad is bound to happen; this is the calm before the storm.

b. This is great, but I wonder if I can keep it up.

c. Finally! My hard work is paying off.

3. You recently broke off a relationship. Which of the following sounds most like something you'd do?

a. Sit on the phone with your closest friend for hours rehashing the relationship. Sometimes you can do this for months.

b. Try to get involved with someone else as quickly as possible.

c. Allow yourself a mourning period. Then move forward, intent on not dwelling in the past or repeating your mistakes.

4. You've lost ten pounds and you have five more to go. What do you do?

a. Dwell on why you just can't get the last five pounds to come off.

b. Buy a new outfit and congratulate yourself; then worry that you won't be able to keep the weight off and how you should be saving money for your retirement.

c. Feel great about the fact that you were able to do something so many people find difficult, and revel in your sense of accomplishment.

5. Your daughter's report card has A's in art and music and a C minus in science. You think:

a. I absolutely have to get her a tutor.

b. I'm going to use art lessons as a reward or punishment for better grades in science.

c. I'll give her extra support in science if she needs it, but I'm proud to have a creative child who excels in the fine arts.

Scoring

Mostly a's and b's? You may see yourself as a realist, but notice whether your thoughts tend to dwell on what's missing instead of what's there. Mostly C's means that you tend to see responsibilities in a balanced way and you don't feel that everything must be on your shoulders.

Is It a Chemical Imbalance?

In our practice we've often seen a simple evaluation dispel fears and bring people a new sense of hope. An objective person can help you confront the underlying questions: Are certain events in your life making you unhappy? Or is the problem your distorted, inner reaction to them, which is something that you can change with some new skills? Could you be suffering from a biochemical imbalance that hasn't been diagnosed?

Harold H. Bloomfield, M.D., and Peter McWilliams offer powerful, empathic words in their book, *How to Heal Depression* (1994):

"You didn't do anything to become depressed. Your failure to do something didn't cause your depression. Depression is an illness. You are no more at fault for having depression than if you had asthma, diabetes, heart disease, or any other illness."

Don't blame yourself. Don't blame anyone else. "Where your depression came from isn't important," Bloomfield and McWilliams maintain, "how to heal it is" (1994, 14).

In the early 1990s, there were exciting breakthroughs in medication for depression that decreased negative thinking and increased energy with a minimum of side effects, and gave people a new sense of hopefulness. Talk to your doctor for more information on these medications. Another excellent resource for understanding the biological components of depression can be found in the first chapter of *The Depression Workbook* by Mary Ellen Copeland (1992).

You have a right to enjoy your own life, to feel alive, to have a vision and the energy to go after it. But if your persistent case of the blues is never dispelled and is always a major part of your life, take it to a therapist who can help you determine what its origin is.

I was once thrown out of a mental hospital for depressing the other patients.

—Oscar Levant

How Much Do We Create Our Own Suffering?

Psychologist and professor Frank Gruba McCalister, who has been studying the subject of suffering for more than a decade, explained in an interview, "Most people cling to the wish that they can be free of suffering. The message that we often receive is that suffering can be conquered by some magical solution, such as some miracle cure or drug, some material possession or some special relationship with another person. All of these eventually prove to be false promises. Because life is a process of constant change, it is also a process of constant loss. For that reason, suffering is an inescapable part of being alive. When we can't accept that, we suffer more (1995)."

McCallister points out that maybe twenty-five percent of life contains this inevitable suffering. The other seventy-five percent we create ourselves. For example, suppose you move into a new apartment, paint your walls, and then notice cracks in the new paint a week later. Anyone would be upset by this. This is McCallister's twenty-five percent. Some people will feel angry, call the insurance company, paint again, because this kind of suffering is a time-limited process that goes away eventually.

But some people will stew and obsess. "I shouldn't have to endure experiences like this. I'm going to sue my landlord. Why do I always end up getting the short end of the stick?" That's the seventy-five percent of self-created suffering. As McCallister puts it, "When we meet suffering with such resistance, we only suffer more. For then we end up suffering because we are suffering (1995)."

Ask yourself: "Is my current unhappiness something that will pass in time if I just accept my feelings? Or is it something that I am ruminating on just out of habit? Am I creating more suffering for myself and others?"

Neurosis is the absence of legitimate suffering.

—Carl Jung

Hidden Payoffs for Staying Unhappy

No one likes to think of themselves as a victim. But if you are often feeling victimized in your life you need to ask yourself a crucial question: Are you trying to get your needs met indirectly? More simply, are you trying to get what you want from other people without having to ask?

Jean is a case in point. She was a woman who complained bitterly about her relationships with driven, self-absorbed men who pursued her and then quickly abandoned her the moment she became emotionally involved.

Jean's father had divorced her mother when she was in junior high. Her mother never admitted that there might have been anything she had done to cause the split and she reviled Jean's father at every opportunity.

Jean saw her mother as a victim. And Jean was sometimes compelled to become other people's victims, as her mother had.

The victim aspect of our personality does its best work in hiding. It loves to pout, plot revenge fantasies, use sarcasm, and hone a whole arsenal of passive-aggressive strategies like "forgetting" to return calls, invalidating compliments, or acting indifferent. These were Jean's strategies and all of them were motivated by her attempts to get her needs met, without having to ask. To ask for anything made her feel too vulnerable.

Below are some of the reasons people tend to be victimized rather than assert themselves directly:

- **You may have been victimized as a child.**

Perhaps you grew up in an environment that was threatening and full of conflict. If you spoke up directly you might have been hit, verbally abused, or abandoned. In the truest sense you were "victimized."

Mary, forty-six, describes her early life history like this: "My father divorced my mother when I was two years old. He remarried, had more children, and I think he felt that I interfered with his desire to forget the past. My mother would always complain that she didn't get enough child support from him. Whenever I asked for anything, she would say I was selfish. But when I began gaining weight in junior high school, and having trouble making friends, then mother would have long conversations with my father and the

child support payment would come on time. I knew it wasn't because he loved me, but because he felt that I was suffering the effects of the divorce."

Unconsciously, Mary came to believe that by remaining unhappy she could "trick the universe" into supplying her with what was due to her in happiness (in material goods, anyway). She fell prey to what therapists refer to as the "just world" theory: if she suffered enough, things would finally equal out.

- **You may be unconsciously trying to protect yourself from more pain.**

As a child, Mary also learned that to deny her own needs and feelings created safety for her. But underneath this strategy of denial she was hurt, angry, and afraid. By not dealing with these emotions, she projected this experience onto the rest of the world, expecting others to treat her as her parents had. She truly believed, *No one will ever really love me* and *Happiness is for other people*. This type of thinking set up a self-fulfilling prophecy as she repeatedly pushed people and opportunities away first, before they could reject her. At times, she would tell the story of her past, and people would respond with empathy and encourage her to deal with her weight problem. Sometimes, someone would offer to take care of her, but, ultimately, all the empathy she received was unsatisfying because it was based on a manipulation rather than being able to really express the truth.

It is important to recognize that this form of self-protection did help her to minimize pain in her childhood. It had survival value for her as a child. But it became her greatest problem in adulthood. What the victim part of most of us needs to do is to speak out, *directly* not indirectly.

Realizing Why It Will Never Be Enough

Here's how one of our clients recently explained the problem: "When I've done something well and someone praises me, I immediately want to push the words away. It's almost superstitious. My fear is, I could get to like praise and compliments and never do anything well again, and then I'd be miserable because there would not be any more praise and compliments."

This client was trying to protect himself from future loss, but at the cost of present happiness. You cannot ward off misery by being miserable. People who are dysthymic or can never feel happy in spite of what they accomplish are people who can't truly affirm themselves. Here are some reasons why:

1. A superstitious feeling that happiness is dangerous.

Kathy says, "My mother can always find a way to be gloomy. She's always saying things like, 'How can you travel when the economy's so bad? What are you going to do about the rainy day when it comes?' I've inherited a lot of this type of thinking to say the least."

Worrying about the rainy day will never be enough for two reasons: When and if it comes, you will still feel the pain. You can't avoid it no matter how prepared you are. Trying to avoid joy so that it won't be followed by a disappointment just means you'll be unhappy when you succeed and unhappy when you are disappointed.

2. A belief that there's always something better out there.

There may be something better somewhere else. Maybe your current success in life is small potatoes relative to your goals. But, we must remind you of an old saying: *Wherever you go, there you are.* If your reaction to success is that it's never enough, you're going to have that feeling when you are at the pinnacle as well as on the journey.

3. A belief that you can get back at people by remaining discontented and unhappy.

"My whole life has been one F-you to my parents," a very bitter client once told us. True, she never gave her family the feeling that they'd done a good job as parents, since in her mind they certainly hadn't. The trouble with this strategy is no matter how miserable you make the people who hurt you, it keeps you mired in negativity and actually more enmeshed with those people. We've conducted family sessions with adult children and their parents where the parents plainly admitted that although they had done their best, it wasn't good enough, and they even apologized. It wasn't enough. The trouble was the adult child had internalized the invalidating, critical parent. "I'll show you," had become, "I'll show me."

4. A belief that not feeling satisfied motivates you to try for bigger and better achievements.

You're the best judge of this. There is, however, absolutely no data that demonstrates that the pessimist achieves higher levels of success than the optimist. In fact, studies show that people who act "as if" they are already where they want to be generally achieve more than those who berate themselves.

> *Almost all your unhappiness in life comes from*
> *your tendency to blame someone else for something.*
>
> —Brian Tracy

Rx: Creating More Happiness in Your Life

Your Key Questions

1. Do I tend to see my life in terms of problems or solutions? Do I generally notice what's right with me and the world or do I focus on what's wrong? How does this affect the quality of my life?
   (E.g., *I am often bitter about what is missing; I rarely appreciate a good time.*)

---

2. What do I fear will happen if I choose to be happy?
   (E.g., *people will criticize me; people will expect me to be happy all the time; people will never take care of me again.*)

---

3. Am I holding on to any unexpressed feelings (anger, sadness, hurt, fear, guilt)?
   (E.g., *I am angry at my father for not being around; I am sad that my family is not very close; I am afraid that my life won't get any better.*)

_____

_____

_____

4. What's good about my life? What am I grateful for?
   (E.g., *I am basically in good health; I have enough money to pay my bills; I have a few good friends; I love my garden.*)

_____

_____

_____

_____

_____

_____

_____

See How Your Symptoms Serve You

Symptom	Protective Function
1. Constantly focusing on problems	1. The hope of finding solutions. Bonding with others in a problem-focused family.
2. Self-criticism	2. To criticize yourself before others do. An attempt at self-improvement.
3. Superstitious thinking	3. To "ward off evil." Fearing good news will lead to catastrophe.
4. Depression	4. You may avoid your uncomfortable feelings by retreating into depression.
5. Guilt	5. You beat yourself up before others do and perpetuate your low self-esteem because it's familiar.
6. Suffering	6. You may feel there is some inherent virtue in your own pain.

Creating New Choices

- "I feel if I get really excited about something, it won't happen."

- "How happy can you get over a five percent raise?"

- "I was happy to get so many clients when I started my consulting business, but now I'm miserable because I don't have the free time I used to have."

Are there any new choices here for unlocking the prison of this type of chronic dissatisfaction?

Exercise: Finding New Solutions

Directions

In column 1, write the symptoms you identified in the section, "See How Your Symptoms Serve You" above.

In column 2, write the original protective function of this strategy.

In column 3, write what is the down side to this solution.

In column 4, describe what would be a more effective solution to this problem.

Example

Symptom	Protective Function	Downside to This Solution	New Choices
When I succeed I can always find something to complain about.	Bonding with other negative thinkers, eliciting their empathy, sometimes a way to motivate myself by saying it's never enough.	Keeps me depressed, frustrated and angry.	Acknowledge what's right, even small successes. Realize that my negative thinking hurts me more than anyone else.
I have fears that if I am too happy, people will resent me or something bad will happen.	Avoid conflict with others. Allay superstitious fears that if I feel good the "other shoe will drop."	I never allow myself to feel happiness.	Understand that this is an outdated and inaccurate protective strategy. Share excitement with a supportive person and see what happens.

Now it's your turn.

Symptom	Protective Function	Downside to This Solution	New Choices
1.			
2.			
3.			
4.			

End the Family Legacy of Negativity

The pessimist sees the difficulty in every opportunity; the optimist,
the opportunity in every difficulty.

—L. P. Jacks

You've got to recognize the family legacy of negativity to untangle yourself from it. Awareness is essential here. People don't always see the negativity in their families, because they're so entrenched in the relationships.

One of our clients told us that his parents had pejorative nicknames for everyone in the family: "Your cousin Harry the Loser; your Uncle Kerry the Cheapskate." It was a family pattern to define people by their flaws and he hated it. He was still surprised to

find that this was the way he tended to define himself: "I am the short one; the one who never finished college; the one who can't afford a down payment on a house."

Criticism of others begets self-criticism. This man no longer involves himself in family "roasts" of other family members. He also works hard to catch himself in his own tendency to be critical of others.

In the next exercise, choose five events that happened to you in the last week. Then, write any negative reaction to it. In the third column, write a positive perspective of this event.

Examples

Event	Negative Perspective	Positive Perspective
1. My friend Joe sold his new book to a top publisher.	He's not so smart. Why doesn't anything that good ever happen to me?	Good for him. I hope he has more success. If I keep working and believing in myself, my time will come too!
2. It's raining out.	Another ruined day! Why does this always happen when I have plans to go outside?	Today I can finish up those tasks I've wanted to complete like the laundry and writing letters. I'll feel less guilty about undone chores and be able to enjoy the sun when it comes out.
3. Judy and Rob are getting married.	It'll probably never work out . . . She's too needy and he's too controlling.	I wish them happiness. Everyone deserves to be happy. My time will come for a good relationship.

It's your turn.

Event	Negative Perspective	Positive Perspective
1.		
2.		

Taking Control of Your Negative Thoughts

We either make ourselves miserable or we make ourselves strong.
The amount of work is the same.

—Castaneda's Don Juan

When we learn problem-focused thinking at an early age, it becomes a habit. Without knowing it, our minds are drawn to negative thoughts the way that metal is attracted to a magnet.

The following exercise is a powerful tool for increasing awareness of your negative thought patterns and will help you retrain your mind to find positive alternatives through intention and self-discipline.

Exercise: Transforming Your Negative Thinking Through Attention and Discipline

For the next seven days you will go on an expedition to hunt down and transform your negative thoughts. Every time you find yourself focusing and dwelling on a negative thought, you have one minute to realize this and shift your thinking away from this problem-focused rumination. If you are unable to refocus yourself in this time, you must start the exercise from the beginning.

Example: "I'm tired. If only I lived in the islands where I could lie on the beach all day.... If only I was born in a wealthy family like Jerry then I'd be happy.... What a drag going to work is ... it will never get any better.... STOP! I'M ON A NEGATIVE THOUGHT CYCLE—Oh who cares? ... I'm depressed.... BUT I DON'T WANT TO KEEP DOING THIS! ... But life sucks.... NO LET'S TURN THIS AROUND.... TAKE A DEEP BREATH ... STRETCH.... Okay—think about something more positive.... Let's see.... Well, I'm taking control right now ... That's pretty cool.... Yes ... I do have a lot going for me.... My health ... my job isn't that bad.... Of course I love getting together with my friends and playing cards.... Now, that's better."

Reclaiming Your Emotions

Exercise: Taking Your Emotional Inventory— "What You Feel You Can Heal"

Our emotions are our most direct and useful indicators of who we are. When we learn to listen to, identify, and understand the messages behind our feelings, they can be our compass in navigating the waters of life.

You may be trying to protect yourself or to restore a sense of order by shutting down emotions. To regain the feeling of being truly alive, to rebuild a sense of hope, the first thing many of us have to do is get back in touch with our emotions and then to express them. Then we will no longer feel so frustrated. We won't feel like victims, or like those

who have little control over events. Simply saying, "This is what I feel; this is what I believe, right or wrong," can restore a sense of control.

For one week score how often you feel each of these emotions on a scale of 1–10 (10 being the most frequent):

Negative Feelings	Mon.	Tues.	Wed.	Thurs.	Fri.	Sat.	Sun.	Total
1. Hurt								
2. Fear								
3. Anger								
4. Sadness								
5. Guilt								
6. Shame								
7. Loneliness								
8. Depression								
Positive Feelings	**Mon.**	**Tues.**	**Wed.**	**Thurs.**	**Fri.**	**Sat.**	**Sun.**	**Total**
9. Love								
10. Gratitude								
11. Excitement								
12. Curiosity								
13. Determination								
14. Playfulness								
15. Pride								
16. Flexibility								

Do not judge your answers, just notice your tendencies. Self-awareness is always the first step to change.

Scoring

Numbers 1–8: Add up your scores for the first eight emotions. If in any of these rows of feelings you score over 35, you will need to focus on these eight. In the next section we will discuss what the eight primary emotions of pain mean.

Numbers 9–16: If any of these rows of feelings fall under a total of 35; you are probably disconnected from these positive feelings in your life. You need to examine your beliefs about embracing these positive emotions thoroughly.

I imagine one of the reasons people cling to their hates so stubbornly is because they sense, once the hate is gone, they will be forced to deal with the pain.

—James Baldwin

Understanding Your Emotions

When a client tells us, "I feel miserable, I just can't seem to get any joy out of anything," we often say, "What do you mean by 'miserable'?" Some clients look at us as if to say, "What on earth are you talking about?" That's because people often label their emotions without fully understanding what these labels mean.

The following definitions will help you understand more clearly some of your most frequently felt emotions.

Hurt Indicates Pain in the Present

Hurt is often experienced as sadness or disappointment.

Key Questions: What was the hurt? Am I willing to be honest with myself about what caused it and voice this to another, in such a way that I will be understood?

Anger Indicates Hurt in the Past

Key Questions: Who hurt me, how and what do I need from them?

Fear (Anxiety) Indicates Real or Imagined Pain in the Future

Key Questions: What am I afraid of and what can I do to create safety? Are my beliefs about this fear irrational?

Guilt Indicates a Feeling That I Did Something Wrong

I violated my own code of ethics. (**Note:** this code may have been internalized from an unhealthy source.)

Key Questions: How can I make amends or modify my code to create a healthier ethical system?

Shame Indicates a Feeling, "There Is Something Wrong with Me"

Key Questions: Where did I learn this? How can I learn to love and accept myself?

Depression Can Indicate a Retreat from Feelings

Key Question: What feelings am I afraid to express and why?

Loneliness Indicates a Lack of Connection

Key Questions: Who or what do I need to connect with? Am I connected with my own needs, desires, and emotions?

Healthy Ways to Handle Feelings

You can learn to see your emotions as your compass designed to help you navigate through your life. As you become clearer at identifying and expressing your feelings, you will find your self-esteem increases, your relationship issues will become clearer, and your self-defeating patterns will become much easier to understand and change. The following guidelines will help.

- Use your feelings as messengers to help you make decisions.

- When you feel mad, or scared, or hurt, ask yourself: "What is this about?" and "What do I need?"

- Take responsibility for being the source of all of your feelings.

- Don't use your feelings to manipulate others (e.g., crying to avoid hearing important feedback about yourself, or getting angry as a way of changing the subject).

- Stay current in the expression of your feelings and don't store them up.

- Learn to view your emotions as friends instead of enemies to be denied or avoided.

- Remember that "what you feel you can heal."

- There are no "bad" feelings and there is an important purpose for each feeling.

*When you hold resentment toward another, you are bound to that person
or condition by an emotional link that is stronger than steel.*

—Catherine Ponder

Developing Empathy for Yourself

Compassion for myself is the most powerful healer of them all.

—Theodore Isaac Rubin, M.D.

One of the most difficult things about being a person who is always dissatisfied is that all you hear from others is a hundred reasons why you *should* be happy. Chances are good that you often lecture yourself on this topic. The trouble is, it almost never works.

Beyond actual physical safety, probably the greatest need we have as children is to be really listened to when we speak and to be responded to with empathy or sympathy. Empathy is an acknowledgment of our true feelings, needs, and thoughts—even when these are negative. As simple as this may sound, it is much less common than you might think. Often we confuse advice with empathy or sympathy.

Consider the following example:

Jeff: I feel too depressed today to go out to dinner.

Mary: Oh honey, stop it. Look at all the wonderful things you have going for you! A great job. Three wonderful children. We have a terrific house. Why be depressed?

Jeff: I think I'll lie down.

In the example above, Mary was clearly trying to be supportive and help Jeff feel better. But was she effective? Mary didn't give her husband a real chance to feel understood or to safely express and clarify his inner struggle.

Let's look at an empathic response.

Jeff: I feel too depressed to go out.

Mary: What's bothering you?

Jeff: I don't know . . . I hate these long winters . . . the sun never comes out.

Mary: I hate that too . . . gray skies all day long.

Jeff: Yeah! I get angry that nine months of every year I have to deal with this cold and gloomy weather.

Mary: I can understand that.

Jeff: Do you think we might talk about moving to a warmer climate?

Mary: Sounds good to me ... maybe we can make a plan.

Jeff: Great! I feel better already. Maybe we can go out for a while if it doesn't turn into an all-night thing.

If you look closely at the two examples, you can see Mary attempting to solve the problem in both cases. However, in the second example, she really listened to Jeff's struggle first and let him express and clarify his feelings. As a result he felt better, and more in the mood to compromise.

Developing empathy is a skill. You may not be able to train other people to be empathic, but ask yourself if you have any real empathy for yourself. If we treat ourselves with little or no empathy, why should anyone else want to give us the understanding we need?

You can practice this with your important relationships. Here's how:

Be Empathic with Yourself

To have empathy for ourselves requires that we stand outside ourselves for a moment, metaphorically speaking, and view ourselves as an understanding, less emotionally attached person would.

Learn a new way of talking to yourself. First listen, without trying to change what you feel. If you can feel what you actually are feeling, and identify that feeling, you can explore it in a more insightful way and move beyond it. Here are a few examples. Keep in mind that an empathic response is not advice. It's not a quick fix. It's an emotional release.

PROBLEM
"This dress is tight. I've gained five pounds and no matter what I do, I can't take the weight off."

Unempathic response
"I look fine. The dress looks great." (Even if it's true, *if you don't believe it*, it doesn't matter how much you say it to yourself.)

"I've got to go out and exercise. I'm so lazy. I've got to stop eating all that red meat." (Now you not only feel fat, you feel inadequate. Not very motivating, is it?)

Empathic response
"It's difficult to not be able to control my weight. I have every reason to feel frustrated."

PROBLEM
"I'm so depressed."

Unempathic response
"That's ridiculous, look at all the reasons I have to be happy." (Perhaps this is true, but what we know intellectually and what we feel emotionally can be two different things).

"You've got to go out more. You've got to meet some new people. Stop feeling sorry for yourself." (Now you not only feel depressed, but foolish and ashamed of your self-pity.)

Empathic response

"It's frustrating to feel depressed, and it seems unfair to feel this way when I can't point to a reason for my feelings. What do I need?"

PROBLEM

"I'm so angry, I could scream."

Unempathic response

"No one cares no matter how much I scream." (They care; they just defend themselves against criticism the way most human beings do.)

"Get a grip on yourself." (What we resist, persists.)

Empathic response

"I'm human. It's frustrating not to get what I want. It's a burden to go through my life feeling that I always have to be fair when other people break the rules."

Now it's your turn to practice empathic responses to your own problems.

Problem	Empathic Response
1. My family takes me for granted.	
2. It's so frustrating. There's never enough money!	
3. I can't seem to get motivated to finish anything. I feel inadequate.	
4. Why do I always have to pick up the phone and call everyone? People use me to make all the plans.	

Go on a Positive Mental Diet

Joy enters the room. It settles tentatively on the windowsill,
waiting to see whether it will be welcome here.

—Kim Chernin

What you focus on expands. If you are looking for more positive feelings to arise in your life, you must begin with a vision, follow it up with positive thoughts, and positive emotions soon will begin to surface. The following exercise is geared to helping you experience more pleasure.

The Emotions of Pleasure

- Excitement

- Gratitude

- Love

- Curiosity

- Determination

- Playfulness

- Pride

1. The first step in creating more positive emotional energy is to know what you are looking for. Memorize the names of the eight emotions of pleasure. Keep a list of them in your wallet or purse, or tape them to your bathroom mirror. Think about them every chance you get.

2. Each day pick a specific emotion on which to focus.

   - Ask yourself: "How can I experience this feeling more fully in my life?"

   - Notice any resistance that comes into your awareness.

   - What thoughts are blocking the full experience of this emotion? (E.g., "How can I feel excited with all the suffering there is in the world?")

   - Find the flaw in this belief and debate it. ("My depression does not solve anyone else's suffering. My positive energy may even help others to feel good.")

3. Drown out the critic with affirmations. In the left column, repeat the affirmation using the positive emotion of your choice. In the right column, let your critic express his/her response. The more you let the critic express itself, the softer it will become. Make copies of this chart to practice with other positive feelings.

Example

Positive Affirmation	Critic's Response
1. I choose to feel *playfulness* today.	1. I'm not a playful person.
2. I choose to feel *playfulness* today.	2. Why bother?
3. I choose to feel *playfulness* today.	3. It's easier to feel depressed.
4. I choose to feel *playfulness* today.	4. I'm still bitter.
5. I choose to feel *playfulness* today.	5. It might be nice.

6. I choose to feel *playfulness* today.	6. It's so hard.
7. I choose to feel *playfulness* today.	7. I'd really like that.
8. I choose to feel *playfulness* today.	8. Will I have to give up my anger?
9. I choose to feel *playfulness* today.	9. I would be happier.
10. I choose to feel *playfulness* today.	10. I choose to feel playfulness today.

Now it's your turn.

Positive Affirmation	Critic's Response
1. I choose to feel _____ today.	1.
2. I choose to feel _____ today.	2.
3. I choose to feel _____ today.	3.
4. I choose to feel _____ today.	4.
5. I choose to feel _____ today.	5.
6. I choose to feel _____ today	6.
7. I choose to feel _____ today.	7.
8. I choose to feel _____ today.	8.
9. I choose to feel _____ today.	9.
10. I choose to feel _____ today.	10.

4. Let a trusted friend know what you are working on. Develop a family of positive emotional support. (You may notice that your current relationships may be stuck in negative thinking!)

5. What goes around comes around. The more positive energy you send out, the more positive energy will come back to you.

6. Humor can be an instant door to positive emotions. Rent a funny movie or go to a comedy club. Watching Robin Williams, Rodney Dangerfield, or Jerry Seinfeld do their routines might be a good start.

Learn a good joke and tell it to someone. You can start with this one:

What did the Zen student say to the hot dog vendor?
"Make me one with everything!"

Your life will reflect back your belief system. *If you want to have a positive life it is imperative that you feed your mind positive thoughts.*

Here are some suggestions for positive activities to feed your mind:

- Read uplifting books

- Associate with positive people

- Listen to motivational tapes

- Listen to inspiring music

- Do aerobic exercise

- Meditate by yourself or with others

- Listen to guided imagery tapes

- Sing or dance

- Compliment others

- Ask others for acknowledgment

- Go for an adventure into nature

Get out of your head and come to your senses.

—Fritz Perls

Keep a Gratitude Journal

You may notice that thoughts of gratitude can be a rare occurrence. This does not mean that there is little to feel grateful about. It means that for many of the reasons we have discussed in this chapter, our thinking does not lead us in that direction.

Gratitude begins with an intention. We need to make a decision to see the light rather than the darkness. The world has no shortage of amazing things for which to be grateful. The sunrise, stars, trees, birds, rivers, oceans, our amazing brains, hands, legs, breathing, vision, colors, music, art, love, emotions, relationships, houses, coffee, fresh fruit, cats, dogs, rabbits, on and on and on.

Exercise

For the next two weeks keep a gratitude journal. This means every day write down five things for which you are grateful.

Here is an excerpt from Mark's journal to use as a model.

Sunday October 1:

1. I am grateful for my health.

2. I am grateful for my marriage.

3. I am grateful for the beauty of nature.

4. I am grateful for my cat.

5. I am grateful for my stereo.

Monday October 2:

1. I am grateful for my condo.

2. I am grateful for my fingers.

3. I am grateful for music.

4. I am grateful for the river outside my house.

5. I am grateful for my friends.

Acknowledging Yourself!

In your journey to greater satisfaction you will need to learn to notice and affirm the positive experiences in your life. Note that if you are a problem-focused thinker, this exercise may be difficult. Keep trying.

Exercise: Five Things I Will Affirm Myself for Today

For the next four weeks keep a journal beside your bed. Each evening review your day and write down five things that you can acknowledge yourself for today. Be creative and don't be skimpy.

Here are some examples:

I made it to work on time ... I worked out today ... I was conscious of my negative thoughts ... I felt more optimistic ... I signed up for a tennis class ... I told my wife that I love her ... I appreciated my health ... I spent twenty minutes listening to a relaxation tape ...

Be Careful Not to Discount Yourself with "But ..."

Initially, it may be very difficult for you to accept a compliment from yourself or others. We often "soften" this acknowledgment by saying "yeah but ..."

Examples

1. I worked out three times this week, but I could have pushed harder.

2. I got up at 7:00 as I promised myself I would, but I was sluggish in the morning.

3. I did my best on that job interview, but I could have been better.

4. I made sure Sean did his homework, but I might be too hard on him.

Notice that when you end a sentence on a negative, it tends to override and discount your positive intention.

Try reversing the order of the two phrases.

Examples

1. I could have pushed harder, but I worked out three times this week.

2. I was sluggish in the morning, but I got up at 7:00 as I promised myself I would.

3. I might have been better on the job interview, but I did give it my best.

4. I was a little hard on Sean, but he did his homework.

Do More of What You Love

> *Most of the time I don't have much fun.*
> *The rest of the time I don't have any fun at all.*
>
> —Woody Allen

It sounds so simple, yet so many of us do not take the time to identify and initiate activities that bring us happiness and satisfaction.

Peter, a thirty-seven-year-old businessman, reminisces, "I think the most fun I ever had was playing first base on my sixth-grade softball team. Getting out there and throwing the ball, the team spirit, the fresh air. I just had the greatest time." When asked when he last played baseball, he responded, "About twenty-five years ago".

You too may be denying yourself some of your greatest pleasures. The following imagery exercise will help you get in touch with some of the pleasures you may have experienced earlier in your life.

Exercise: Guided Visualization—Childhood Play

Begin this exercise by finding a quiet place where you will not be disturbed for at least twenty minutes. Now take a few deep breaths and close your eyes.

Imagine yourself breathing in relaxation and breathing out tension. . . . With each breath feel a wave of relaxation come through your body. . . . See yourself at the top of a beautiful staircase with ten steps. . . . Design this staircase anyway you like . . . As you slowly walk down, you feel calmer and more relaxed as you go deeper and deeper into a

wonderful state of relaxation. . . . Calmer and calmer. . . . Your body feels heavier as your muscles let go and feel limp and relaxed. . . . Imagine a golden light passing through your body, filling you with a sense of peace and contentment. . . . As you arrive at the bottom of the staircase you open a door to your past. . . .

Now go back to a time in your childhood when you can recall yourself doing a very enjoyable activity . . . something that brought you a great amount of pleasure. . . . See this scene as clearly as you can . . . Using all your senses, smell the air, see your surroundings in as much detail as possible, hear the sounds, tune into your feelings. . . . Spend a few minutes reliving the experience. . . . Now go back to another moment in your personal history . . . Relive it using all your senses: smell the air, hear the sounds, feel the emotions, see the surroundings in detail . . . When you are done slowly open your eyes.

Now in your journal, write a list of these pleasurable experiences and think about how you can add these experiences to your adult life today. We've started the list with some examples. You can fill in the blanks.

Pleasurable Experiences in Childhood	How Can I Add These to My Adult Life Today?
1. Poker games with friends in high school	1. Set up card games with friends now
2. Art class in eighth grade	2. Take adult education class in painting
3. Going to a Saturday matinee	3. Going to a Saturday movie
4. After school sports	4. Join a softball league
5.	5.
6.	6.
7.	7.
8.	8.
9.	9.
10.	10.

Satisfying Activities List

Playing golf	Playing Monopoly
Knitting	Rereading a childhood book
Going to a botanical garden	Organizing my desk
Finding a Waterslide park	Singing
Building a website	Buying a new game

Clay sculpting

Taking a dance class

Buying a pet

Going to the beach

Meditating

Volunteer work

Daily affirmations

Building a model

Going to an amusement park

Listening to music

Doing nothing

Sex

Playing baseball

Barbecue

Some other activities I like to do:

_____

_____

_____

_____

_____

_____

My commitment this week

I, _____ , will add the following three activities to my life:

1. _____

2. _____

3. _____

Exercise: Creating Adventure Days

Your task: Create an adventure list and then one day each week go out on a personal adventure.

Here's a sample adventure list:

1. Drive through the Colorado mountains.

2. Get great tickets to the Bulls game.

3. Explore a new part of the city I live in.

4. Explore parts of the East Coast I've never seen.

5. Go on a meditation retreat.

6. Take a trip to a botanical garden.

7. Go on a river-rafting trip.

8. Find a new bicycle path and explore it.

9. Take a cooking class.

10. Find a waterfall (and build a home there).

My Adventure List

1. _____

2. _____

3. _____

4. _____

5. _____

6. _____

7. _____

8. _____

9. _____

10. _____

Light Therapy

Everyone experiences mood fluctuations as the seasons change. Yet for some the changes are severe and reflect a syndrome known as Seasonal Affective Disorder (SAD). SAD affects some thirty-five million Americans; some estimates report as many as one in every four people.

SAD will show up as a recurring fall-winter depression marked by feelings of blues, agitation, moodiness, lethargy, or fatigue. These symptoms can also include a change in sleeping and eating patterns.

Research has linked the SAD symptoms with the lack of exposure to light in the months from November to March. Chicago, for example, which has 220 hours of sun in an average June dwindles to a skimpy eighty hours of sunlight in December.

Will Any Kind of Light Do?

The traditional desk lamp shines at the rate of 300 lux (a unit used to measure brightness), while the light of the sun at noontime radiates about 150,000 lux. In the 1980s, scientists devised a portable light for light therapy that radiates about 10,000 lux. When tested

with patients with Seasonal Affective Disorder or depressive disorders, their symptoms started to improve. One patient reported, "Sitting next to this light for forty-five minutes to one hour a day helps me feel less depressed, more alert, and energetic."

Is It Just for SAD?

Using light therapy for a period of time can help other problems too. Corporate jet travelers have found that light boxes help with jet lag and traveling stress, depression, and fatigue. In fact, as research continues, it is becoming clear that most people can benefit from a good dose of light.

Exercise

Is the lack of light in your life influencing your negative thinking or your inability to be happy for long?

Write out your thoughts on this subject and describe any examples that come to mind.

_____

_____

_____

_____

New Thoughts and New Actions

Not everything that is faced can be changed;
but nothing can be changed until it is faced.

—James Baldwin

Positive Affirmations You Can Say to Yourself

- If I focus on my positive moments and enjoy them fully, I'll have the energy to create more of them.

- My current unhappiness doesn't pay other people back for the past.

- I will be as kind and understanding to myself as I would for a best friend.

- Holding on to bitterness only creates more of it.

- I choose to let go of it now.

- One flaw in my performance doesn't make me a failure.

- I will appreciate today as if it is my last.

- Misery is not a lucky charm that protects me from bad luck.

- Today, I will realize that I have the right to be happy. The past is over. I can change my perceptions in this moment.

- I am lovable, capable, and beautiful just the way I am.

- Love is letting go of fear. As I open my heart and emotions, I will find others more loving toward me.

- Each day I feel more positive about myself and realize that I am taking control of my life.

Positive Things You Can Do for Yourself

- Don't store up your emotions. Tell people in a reasonable way how they upset you so you don't turn your anger inward into depression or anxiety.

- Instead of rehashing your mistakes, acknowledge your small successes (getting your assignment in on time, writing in this workbook, taking time to relax) on a daily basis.

- Find ways to fulfill the needs that were not met in your childhood. Allow yourself to accept nurturing and affirmation.

- Get out of your head and into your body. Find fun activities (go to the park, play catch, plant a garden).

- Be direct about what you want from others.

- Bring more humor into your life. Collect jokes, watch funny movies and TV shows.

- See criticism as feedback, be careful not to blow it out of proportion. Watch out for cognitive distortions such as "all or nothing thinking" or "tunnel vision."

- Spend time each day asking and answering the question: "What's right with my life?"

- Reparent your inner child by speaking to yourself in loving and empathic ways, as you would to a real child.

4

When You Can't Stop Comparing Yourself to Other People

*The Third Key: Identity—
Gaining a Clear Understanding
of Who You Really Are and
the Confidence to Be Yourself*

Understanding the Key Issue

June stands in the locker room at her health club and rummages through her workout bag for her combination lock. She's kept her commitment to a three-times-a-week exercise

schedule for more than five weeks. But for all the motivation it took, the club is giving her little satisfaction today. She's brought her friend Megan with her as a guest and even before it's begun the exercise session is turning out to be a nightmare.

"Are you doing any yoga?" Megan asks her as she wriggles her body into her tights. "There's a great class on Saturday mornings at my club. And weights. You've got to do some weights." June can't help but notice that Megan doesn't have an ounce of fat on her. *Where does she get the time?* June wonders. She tries not to stare at her friend, but she can't help but see that Megan's body is toned everywhere. *Compared to her, I'm fat,* June thinks, depressed.

Or consider Ron's situation. Ron and his wife are arguing. "We don't need a new car," she tells him, her voice beginning to rise. "We just bought this house. We can't handle another loan payment."

"You don't commute two hours a day, so how would you know about cars?" he shouts back. "Besides, there's a problem with the carburetor."

"The carburetor was fine, until your brother bought a Lexus," his wife counters. Ron, stung, leaves the room.

Sara has an entirely different issue. She's been arguing with her mother for several weeks.

"Mom, don't make such a big deal out of this," Sara finally says, exasperated.

"Shouldn't a mother make a big deal when her only daughter gets a master's degree?" her mother replies, sounding hurt.

But Sara can never make her mother understand. Her degree is from a local university, the only one that was affordable. Most of her friends have MBAs that they got right after college from top schools in the nation. It took her six years to finish her degree, and in the last year she's begun to wonder what the hard work was all about. She can't get enthusiastic about the graduation party her mother wants to plan. Compared to everyone else's, her graduation doesn't seem like such a big deal.

At a time when Sara, Ron, and June could have been happy, they were feeling miserable. No matter what they had accomplished—no matter what goals they had met, when they compared themselves to others—it always seemed like it wasn't enough.

Most people compare themselves to others at times. Our society encourages competition, moving up, and above all, "keeping up with the Joneses." It can be motivating to have role models and mentors who stand further along the path and from whom one can learn, but it can also be debilitating and depressing.

June's comparison of her body to her more tightly toned friend's caused her to feel frustrated at a time when she had good reason to feel satisfied with her commitment to her health and to staying trim. Eventually, she quit working out. Sara, who thinks her MBA is trivial compared to her friends' degrees, finds herself anxious, focused on negativity, and wrapped up in the notion that other people of equal talent have passed her by. The result is that potential employers put as low a value on her skills as she does because she minimizes them so much. Ron's competition with his more successful older brother is a family legend. He's even ashamed that he secretly wishes his brother would fail once in a while.

If you are constantly comparing yourself to others and the comparisons make you miserable, why do you do it? Let's take a look at what creates such a behavioral pattern.

Discovering the Roots of Your Struggle

> *My family was so dysfunctional that I thought that yelling, screaming,*
> *hitting each other, and hiding in the closet were normal.*
>
> —Terry Kellog

The Number One reason people compare themselves with others is because our culture encourages such comparative thinking. However, in our experience, there are definitely some other reasons why some people get stuck so deeply in that particular pattern that they never feel happy with themselves or their lives. Some of those are as follows:

- Growing up with a family secret that makes you feel different from everyone else

- Competing in school environments that had little tolerance for average or below-average performance

- Growing up in a family that discounted your needs and feelings

- Being influenced by advertising that constantly encourages us to compare ourselves with the richest, brightest, and most beautiful people

Growing Up Feeling "Different"

Most children usually wish to conform, to fit in and be like everyone else. What happens when it's obvious that you or your family are different from most of the other children and their families? Consider some of the following instances from our files:

My father had a mild case of Parkinson's disease. The tremor wasn't terrible, but it was obvious. The medical bills drained most of the money my parents had. Our home looked nice on the outside but inside it was falling apart. Even my little sister, at seven, knew how to hit the furnace with a hammer in a certain spot, to make it start working. So, yes, I did feel different in a neighborhood where hired gardeners trimmed lawns and women who spoke little English traveled an hour on the bus to clean the houses.

My mother died when I was five. I think my father married the first woman he could after my mother's death because he couldn't cope with raising three kids by himself. Our stepmother hated us. She once told us that we killed our mother by being so noisy and selfish. She was a mean-spirited person who searched through our drawers, or woke us up in the middle of the night to punish us because our room was messy. But we never told anyone what was going on, except an aunt, who just shook her head and told us to hang in there, get good grades, and get scholarships so we could move away.

I was a very heavy child. I wore baggy clothes, thinking it would make me look thinner, but I know people looked at me, and made snide remarks that I couldn't

hear. I lost the weight when I was in high school, but I never lost the feeling that I was fat.

I grew up in a quiet suburb of Los Angeles in the 1950s. Our house was smaller than most, in a wealthy community that prided itself in showing well to the neighbors. On the surface, our family was able to hold its own by presenting our best selves to the public while we kept the dirty laundry hidden behind closed doors. My brothers and I were given our own cars at sixteen, while my father had to juggle the checkbook each month to make the mortgage payment on the house. But he wanted us to have what the other kids had.

At night I would hear my parents arguing in their bedroom about how little money we had and how indulgent my father was about giving the kids almost anything they wanted. I was never sure where we stood with money. My dad would give me twenty dollars and my mother would complain that we couldn't pay the grocery bills. Twenty-five years later, money is still a confusing issue for me. My mother was a master of presenting the perfect image to the outside. My parents would scream at each other at the dinner table to the point where my mother would turn purple. Then if the phone rang, she would pick it up and without any hesitation say cheerfully, "Oh. Elaine, Hi. No, I wasn't busy. I was just thinking about you!" One message was clear: "Don't ever let anyone outside the family know the truth."

The particular secret that makes you feel different from everyone else during your childhood may be a family divorce, an illness, a financial problem, an addiction, or a pair of parents at war with each other. It can be even more subtle such as reaching puberty early or not being able to memorize the multiplication tables, or personal terror—of the water, of a flying baseball, of undressing in front of others.

The only criterion that makes it a secret is that you are told not to tell anyone outside the family what's going on. "We understand that you have trouble with math, dear, but don't let Aunt Betty know you have to go to summer school." Or "Don't let the other kids know you're scared—just go out there and act like you know what you're doing."

Sometimes we're forced to keep the family secret to protect our parents so they won't endure a loss of face. But sometimes it's because they don't want us to be hurt. "You're the same as everyone else, and don't let anyone tell you you're not," they remind us. But if that's true, why not just talk openly about what's going on? Why hide it?

If you identify with these issues, you might wonder, "What does having a family secret have to do with constantly comparing yourself with others twenty years later?" The answer is that keeping a family secret during childhood can be the beginning of a lifelong pattern of feeling isolated. If you can't openly share yourself with others, you must learn to avoid closeness. In a very basic sense, you begin to feel left out, isolated, "different." You may try to hide your vulnerabilities by competing, but such a strategy is more isolating.

You see only the surface of other people's lives as they are allowed to see only the surface of yours. As a result, you feel comparatively lessened. You worry about being found out or found lacking. Comparison thinking becomes the way you seek to protect yourself. *Comparison thinking* occurs when you try to measure or grade your standing in

comparison to everyone else's, on a scale of value that is not visible to anyone but you. It also becomes important that you are never "found out" making these comparisons.

A lie would make no sense, unless the truth were felt to be dangerous.

—Carl Jung

Identifying Your Family Secrets

What were your family secrets? Think for a moment. How did you feel your home differed from other children's homes as you grew up? What weren't you supposed to speak openly about? How did this make you feel? Place a checkmark next to each secret you can relate to. Add your own secrets at the bottom of the list.

My Secrets

Our family was always in financial trouble.	✓
One or both of my parents were alcoholic.	
My parents were divorced.	
I lied about my school grades.	✓
I flunked a course in school.	✓
I lied to my friends about small things.	✓
I was caught shoplifting.	
I did a lot of drugs or alcohol and lied about it.	✓
My father/mother used to hit me or other members of my family.	✓
My religious beliefs were different than most other people's in the neighborhood.	
One of my parents had an addiction.	✓
My parents fought a lot.	✓

Perhaps there were no secrets in your family. It's possible that the root of your comparison thinking lies in your school experience. Schools often foster competition through ability grouping, point systems, and class rankings. Do you remember your placement in reading groups or math groups? The level of the high school classes in which you were placed? Do you remember your ACT or SAT score? Your class rank? How does it make you feel to recall these numbers or rankings?

One of our clients is a brilliant artist. When he was growing up he had what today is called Attention Deficit Disorder (ADD) but was then called hyperactivity. "I was definitely out of the box, if you know what I mean. I wasn't interested in sports. I wasn't interested in reading. I just wanted to draw." He still just wants to draw, but he is as critical of his drawing as he is of everything else he does. His fantasy? "I'd like to be an investment banker, so successful I'd have the time to draw, and people would say about me, 'He's so smart, and so creative, too.'" The trouble is, he rarely draws. Because his drawings aren't up to par, as he sees it, he does very little drawing at all.

Exercise: How Competitive Did You Have to Be in School?

List several instances when you compared yourself to other children at school. List whether you compared yourself positively, negatively, or neutrally.

Here's an example of recalling these kinds of incidents from one of our clients.

I Compared Myself	Positively	Negatively	Neutrally
1. I had a better report card than my best friend.	X		
2. I compared my body to other classmates' bodies and I felt embarrassed.		X	

	Positively	Negatively	Neutrally
3. My ACT scores were lower than many of my friends.		X	
4. I was often one of the first kids who were picked for sports teams.	X		
5. I wasn't in the popular group, but I had plenty of friends.			X
6. I didn't start dating as early as my friends did.		X	

To help you get started, think in terms of grades, teams, dating, test scores, physical attributes, athletic or artistic abilities.

I Compared Myself	Positively	Negatively	Neutrally
1.			
2.			
3.			
4.			
5.			
6.			
7.			
8.			
9.			
10.			

Many cultures place an inordinately high value on being the best, the richest, the smartest, the most powerful, the thinnest, or the fastest. Bill Gates is idolized for his wealth, while Cindy Crawford is envied for her looks. We need role models to serve as mentors, to guide us toward realizing a vision of our own best selves, not as impossible ideals against which we make comparisons that lead us only to feelings of inadequacy.

Look at your answers from the previous exercise. Then, repeat the following positive affirmations to yourself:

1. I was a child. I didn't know what I now know, and I did the best I could then.

2. If I wasn't the best, I still had enough conviction to stay in the race.

3. If I made mistakes, I can realize that's what childhood is all about.

4. I was unique and adventurous as a young child; those qualities are still within me.

5. I can learn and grow to develop my unique voice in the world.

"I Wasn't Good Enough"

The words "I am . . ." are potent words; be careful what you hitch them to.
The thing you're claiming has a way of reaching back and claiming you.

—A. L. Kitselman

When we feel that we are different from other people, we sometimes think that we are worse. Often, a sense of shame follows that thought. In the book *Facing Shame* (1986), Fossom and Mason distinguish the difference between guilt and shame:

> A person with guilt might say, "I feel awful seeing that I did something which violated my values." Or the guilty person might say, "I feel sorry for the consequences of my behaviors." In doing so the person's values are reaffirmed. The possibility of repair exists and learning and growth are promoted. While guilt is a painful feeling of regret and responsibility for one's actions, shame is a painful feeling about oneself as a person. The possibility for repair seems foreclosed to the shameful person because shame is a matter of identity, not of behavioral infraction. There is nothing to be learned from it and no growth is opened by the experience because it only confirms one's negative feelings about oneself.

In essence, guilt signifies, *"I did something wrong. I have violated my values."* Shame implies, *"I feel there is something wrong with me."* It is an issue of identity.

John Bradshaw, in his groundbreaking book, *Healing the Shame That Binds You*, defined and discussed the distinction between healthy and toxic shame:

> What I discovered was that shame as a healthy human emotion can be transformed into shame as a state of being. As a state of being, shame takes over one's whole identity. To have shame as an identity is to believe that one's being is flawed, that one is defective as a human being. Once shame is transformed into an identity, it becomes toxic and dehumanizing (1988, vii).

This often stems from the reality of our early life experience when we were sometimes shamed for expressing ourselves. This shame became internalized and subsequently was projected out onto the world.

Note that any "toxic shame" that you may feel isn't obvious to others. This is because a shame-bound person is often a master of disguise. The tremendous fear of exposure underlying shame fuels the creation of a false self.

To feel "healthy shame" as opposed to "toxic shame" is essentially to accept our humanity. This means to realize we are human beings who have limitations and imperfections—and that this is all right. It is the acceptance of just those limitations and imperfections that allows us to break through the binds of toxic shame.

> *Shame is one of the major destructive forces in all human life.*
> *In naming shame, I began to have power over it.*
>
> —John Bradshaw

How does shame develop and take root and lead to comparison thinking? Like many psychological mechanisms, it begins in childhood. Young children are like sponges. They absorb information from their environment about who they are. Through a process called "mirroring" they learn to look to the outer world to reflect back others' thoughts and feelings to consolidate their own sense of identity. In the best of all worlds, this reflection is accurate:

Sara: Mommy, I'm scared.

Mom: It is scary in the dark sometimes. But I'll protect you.

Jack: Mommy, I'm mad at Billy for not meeting me when he said he would.

Mom: I can understand why you're angry. He broke a promise to you.

When this type of mirroring matches our internal truth, we begin to trust our instincts and we accept our feelings as valid. Consider the same examples with faulty shame-based responses:

Sara: Mommy I'm scared.

Mom: (angrily) What's wrong with you? There's nothing to be scared about.

Jack: Mommy, I'm mad at Billy for not meeting me when he said he would.

Mom: No wonder! No one wants to play with a boy with such a messy, dirty room as yours!

Sara learned two things: (1) Her feelings were not to be trusted. (2) She should act older and more like an adult than she actually was ready to do. To avoid upsetting her mom again Sara unconsciously began to repress her feelings, and share less and less with others for fear of being shamed again.

In fact, for Sara a pattern just like this played out in most of her relationships and was paramount by the time she reached the age of thirty-five, when she entered therapy.

Her complaint? "No matter what I accomplish, I never feel it's good enough. Compared to other people I feel like I've achieved nothing." Sara's biggest problem was that she was so focused on who she *should* be that she had little idea who she really was.

Jack also learned that his feelings were not to be trusted. He learned that when he left himself open and vulnerable, this often was a setup for an attack in other areas of his life. Jack grew up wary of others and constantly compared himself to them to get a sense of where he stood and whether or not they could make him feel inferior.

If It Hurts So Much, Why Do It?

We know about comparison thinking from personal experiences. Here's a story about comparison thinking that was very enlightening for one of us (Mitch).

> Ever since I was a little kid I loved music. At the age of fourteen, I started taking guitar lessons and before long in 1966 I joined my first rock and roll band, The Goldfingers. My heroes were The Beatles. My dream was to sing like Paul McCartney.
>
> Even though my guitar playing steadily grew better, my singing didn't. I would sing along with the records, straining to sound like Paul. I got discouraged because I sounded so awful. Finally, I gave up and let the bass player in the band sing all the lead vocals.
>
> Over the years I became a good guitar player, but I always felt frustrated because I couldn't sing. In college, I started a band, Redwood Landing. We recorded an album, and even had a big following, but although I added some low background harmonies, I never had the confidence or ability to pull off lead vocals. As satisfying as my guitar playing was, as many compliments as I got, I always felt that something was missing. Why couldn't I sing like Paul McCartney?
>
> I moved to San Francisco when I hit thirty. One day I went for a vocal lesson with one of the great jazz singers of the day, Mark Murfey. He began the lesson by asking me to sing a song. I started singing "Bye Bye Blackbird." After about thirty seconds he said, "Hold on! Don't you know that key is way too high for you? Can't you feel how much you're straining? Your neck is tight and you're pinching your vocal chords."
>
> I said, "I guess I'm no Paul McCartney!" He replied, "Of course not. He's a tenor and you're a baritone."
>
> I had never given that a moment's thought before. Every band I grew up listening to seemed to have had lead singers who were tenors. I compared my voice with their voices and tried to emulate their sound. No one ever told me that this was the worst thing I could have done.
>
> I lowered the pitch of my voice and started to listen for the strengths in my own unique voice. Over the next few years I learned to relax my throat, support my breathing, and develop my own sound. I improved dramatically. Now at forty-seven, I'm currently recording a CD of my original songs. Instead of finding the best studio singer in Chicago to record them, I am singing my songs in my own voice.

You may have no interest in singing, but I hope the take-home lesson is clear to you: When we try hard to be just like someone else, we often lose our greatest gift, our own voice.

Realizing Why It Will Never Be Enough

When you give up your own truth to win at someone else's game, everyone loses.

—Stephan Paul

Let's consider the reason you compare yourself to others. You probably think comparison will motivate you to achieve more, or become the best you can be. That's an understandable goal. But what goes awry with the whole comparison habit? You focus on other people's unique qualities and try to emulate them. You become a copy, not an original. It's your original take on the world and your unique voice that, once expressed, will give you the satisfaction you can never experience as a "copy."

Suppose that you're a writer who has finally gotten a contract to publish your first novel. You compare yourself with other first-time authors such as yourself. You think, "Well, if they can accomplish that, I might be able to, also." You learn what they did to market their books and increase their sales and you follow suit, or you invent your own strategies.

But suppose, instead, you compare yourself to Stephen King. You have no idea what Mr. King's sales figures were on his first book or whether or not he struggled to get his work recognized in the first place (and he did). All you see is that he's making millions. You publish your book and the sales are respectable, in the range of what most first-time authors accomplish. But you don't feel proud. You don't realize that you may have reached your own separate audience, as large or small as that might be, and affected their lives in a positive way. When your book goes into a second printing of another ten thousand copies, you still feel as if it's very small potatoes.

One client told us, "My self-esteem swings back and forth. I either feel grandiose, like I am this special person destined to change the world, or I feel like a bug, insignificant and only here to be swept up and tossed away. I wonder, often, who am I really?"

The comparison thinker can always find someone better to compare himself/herself against. Here are some realizations about the futility of comparison thinking that some of our clients reached. These insights helped them to understand that the practice of always comparing oneself with others frequently winds up becoming "there's never-enough thinking." Highlight those that apply to your life.

- I've made big and little changes in my life—buying a home, having a child, taking a class, cutting my hair, dressing differently, not because I wanted to do any of these things, but because they had been good moves for somebody else.

- I find myself trying to copy others rather than look to myself and say, "What do you really think?"

- I imagine that everyone who makes more money than me is happier than me.

- I weighed 105 pounds, and I was thinner than I'd ever been, but I still thought my thighs were fat.

- If I surpass someone I've envied, it doesn't really matter. I just find another person to envy.

What would change in your life if you began to see that you were neither the best nor the worst, but essentially like everyone else? What if your dreams could inspire and motivate you rather than discouraging you and causing you to feel inadequate? What would be the result if you realized that the reason you keep comparing yourself to others is that you *lack a clear understanding of who you really are, and the confidence to be yourself*?

If you take the self-affirming risk of learning who you are and learn how to live your uniqueness every day, you can give up comparing yourself to others and chastising yourself for not being like them. Imitations rarely become stars. Your feelings of being different can actually be made to work for you.

The exercises that follow are aimed at helping you find your own voice Once you are comfortable with that voice, once you understand that your own personality is more vital and suited to your strengths than any you could mimic, you will begin to focus less on comparing yourself to others and concentrate more on continuing your unique personal path.

Rx: Finding Yourself

Be yourself. Who else is better qualified?

—Frank J. Giblin II

Your Key Questions

1. What are five qualities I most like about myself? What are five qualities I would like to change?
   (E.g., *likes—my intelligence, my hair, my sensitivity. Changes—my negative thinking, etc.*)

   _____

   _____

   _____

   _____

   _____

2. Am I in touch with my emotions, needs, and values? What can I do to clarify these?
   (E.g., *Keep a journal of emotions; talk to a friend or therapist.*)

   _____

   _____

   _____

   _____

   _____

3. If I concentrated on what I have in common with others instead of how we're different, what would change in my relationships?
   (E.g., *Would I be less competitive, and would I feel less anxiety and less superficiality?*)

   _____

   _____

_____

_____

_____

_____

4. What can I do today to start believing in myself more fully?
   (E.g., *I can think more about the successes in my life; I can affirm my talents and think more about what I want and need.*)

_____

_____

_____

_____

_____

See How Your Symptoms Serve You

Current symptoms are almost always old solutions to past problems and trauma. They worked once, after a fashion, but they don't work for you today.

Examples

Problem	Protective Function
1. Comparing myself to my friends and feeling I'm less.	Avoid pain of criticism by criticizing myself first. Possibly as an attempt at motivating myself. To find out where I stand.
2. Comparing myself to others and feeling superior.	An attempt to improve my self-esteem. An attempt to overcompensate for feelings of inferiority.
3. Comparing myself to celebrities and feeling frustrated because I can't obtain that level of success.	Possible attempt at motivation; also an excuse to give up; i.e., why bother?
4. Avoiding people who I think are better than I am.	Avoiding feelings of shame, criticism, or falling short, not being able to measure up.

People often say that this or that person has not yet found himself. But the self is not something that one finds. It is something that one creates.

—Thomas Szasz

Exercise: Your Costs and Benefits

Make a list of the payoffs you receive for constantly comparing yourself to others.

1. _____
2. _____
3. _____
4. _____
5. _____
6. _____
7. _____
8. _____
9. _____
10. _____

Here's the list that Jackie, thirty-four, made about what she expects to gain by comparing herself to others:

1. I'll know where I stand.

2. I'll be motivated to keep trying to improve myself when I see what others are able to accomplish.

3. I'll feel safe.

4. I'll understand what's normal.

5. It will stop me from being lazy or complacent.

6. It will help me appreciate what I have in comparison to other people.

Jackie found that it was difficult to complete her list. There weren't as many benefits gained from comparing herself to others as she had thought there were. What came up again and again in her thoughts was the notion of protecting herself from being surprised by others, or of feeling inadequate next to them. "I compare myself to other people and use the comparison as a way to avoid people who intimidate me. It's a way to protect myself from being hurt, I guess. If I think I'm not as smart as someone else is, for instance, then I'm not taken by surprise when that really becomes clear to me."

Go back to your list. Put a plus sign beside each payoff that enhances your life. For instance, if you feel that comparing yourself to others truly motivates you, put a plus sign there. If, however, you realize that it really doesn't motivate you, mark a minus sign. Those minus signs point to areas where you can begin shifting your thinking and revising your categories.

Creating New Choices

Choose one to three examples of comparing yourself to others that you believe are currently causing frustration in your life. Then complete the chart below.

- In the first column, write the symptoms you identified in "See How Your Symptoms Serve You."

- In the second column, write the original protective function of this strategy.

- In the third column, write the downside to this solution.

- In the fourth column, write a more effective solution to this problem

Example

Symptom	Protective Function	Downside to This Solution	New Choices
I've avoided my best girlfriend after she married a wealthy man because I can't compete with her money.	If I don't see her, I don't get jealous. I avoid a blow to my self-esteem.	I miss a good friend who made me laugh.	I can stop thinking about how our lives are different and start thinking about where we still connect. I can talk openly to her about this.

Now it's your turn.

Symptom	Protective Function	Downside to This Solution	New Choices
1.			
2.			
3.			

Getting Yourself in Clearer Focus

I've always wanted to be somebody, but I see now I should have been more specific.

—Lily Tomlin

The key to ending painful comparison thinking is to discover that you have something unique and valuable to offer. One powerful technique for self-understanding is the sentence completion exercise. Complete the following sentences with the first thoughts that come to mind. Try not to censor your answers. Your first instincts are often the most accurate. There are no right or wrong answers. If you prefer to use a separate sheet of paper, do so.

1. I feel good about myself when

_____

2. When I look in the mirror I think

_____

3. A skill I am proud of is

_____

4. One thing I regret is

_____

5. One time I was really happy when

_____

6. You'd never guess that I'm

_____

7. I am secretly angry about

_____

8. I am still sad that

_____

9. If I knew I couldn't fail, I would

_____

10. The thing that scares me about intimacy is

_____

11. I know I'm in love when

_____

12. One thing I wish I had more time to do is

_____

13. I'd like to do less of

_____

14. The role I played in my family was

_____

15. I learned from my father that

_____

16. I learned from my mother that

_____

17. No one would ever guess that I

_____

18. One thing that holds me back from feeling happy is

_____

19. The thing I remember most about growing up is

_____

20. If money wasn't an obstacle, the first thing I'd do is

_____

21. One thing I've always meant to do is

_____

22. My teachers usually felt I was

_____

23. One thing I like best about myself is

_____

24. One thing I like least about myself is

_____

25. My best friend would probably describe me as

_____

26. Someone who didn't like me would probably describe me as

_____

27. My mother always said I was

_____

28. My father always said I was

_____

29. Today my family makes me feel

_____

30. I wish more people realized that I am actually very

_____

As you read over your answers, some may surprise you, some may confuse or even alarm you. Some may even make you feel more in touch with yourself. Sometimes clients complete this exercise and judge their own answers, for example, "I didn't know what to say, so I pretty much wrote anything."

We say, "Whatever you wrote, read through it again. Study it. There's a person behind those answers with a definite identity and a unique voice. Give that person a chance."

Don't compromise yourself. You are all you've got.

—Betty Ford

Using Movies, Books, and Songs to See Yourself

One of the best ways to identify our true values, desires, and feelings is to notice the things in our lives that appeal to us. This type of meaning and connection is easily observed through our preferences in the arts. In this exercise you may fill in the blank lines below, or use a separate sheet of paper to answer the following questions. Your answers will "mirror" back to you who you really are.

List five of your favorite movies and explain why they are your favorites.

1. _____

2. _____

3. _____

4. _____

5. _____

Now, list five of your favorite books and explain why they are your favorites.

1. _____

2. _____

3. _____

4. _____

5. _____

Now, list five of your favorite songs and explain why they are your favorites.

1. _____

2. _____

3. _____

4. _____

5. _____

Examples

"One of my favorite movies was *Ordinary People* because it was so similar to my family. I could relate to the troubled teenager who held in all of his feelings. Mary Tyler Moore played a cold detached mother (very familiar) and Donald Sutherland played a wimpy dad who was 'too nice.' I loved the part when the kid went to the therapist and finally let out his true feelings of guilt about his brother's death—I still get chills—I guess I still hold a lot in myself."

"One of my favorite books is *Gone with the Wind*. I also idealized men who weren't right for me just because they were distant and self-involved like Scarlett's love Ashley Wilkes. I had lots of Rhetts in my life who I couldn't appreciate either. I can see that I'm attracted to people who are very different from me because I equate different with better."

"One of my favorite songs is *Deacon Blues* by Steely Dan. It talks about the dark side and the struggle of losing. The chorus goes like this, 'They got a name for the winners in the world, I want a name when I lose. They call Alabama the Crimson Tide, call me Deacon Blues.' But I really love the line, 'I cried when I wrote this song—sue me if I play too long!' I'd love to tell a few people that just once . . . maybe I will."

Clarifying Your Values

Sometimes I wish I could be someone else. Then
I realize the only thing I haven't tried is being myself.

—Anne Wilson Schaef

Another way to get in touch with your true identity is to take a closer look at what you value. Complete the following checklist. After you have filled in your scores for columns 1 and 2, subtract column 2 from column 1 to assess the amount of room you have for growth with this value.

Value	How Important This Value Is to Me (1–10)	How Much I Practice This Value (1–10)	Your Margin for Growth (Subtract column 2 from column 1.)
Freedom			
Honesty			
Relaxation			
Family connections			
Love			
Adventure			
Acceptance of others			
Acceptance of myself			
Emotional availability			
Fitness			
Responsibility			
Vulnerability			
Encouragement			
Happiness			
Trust			

Open communication			
Passion			
Creativity			
Power			
Intelligence			
Spirituality			
Playfulness			
Giving			
Health consciousness			
Artistic qualities			
Gratitude			
Sensitivity			
Risk taking			
Personal growth			

Scoring

Don't look for an answer key here. Your values are not right or wrong, they're simply yours. Use the list primarily to gain more insight into yourself and resist the impulse to concentrate on what others value and how you stack up against them.

Using Role Models to Develop Your Identity

If we go down into ourselves we find that we possess exactly what we desire.

—Simone Weil

If we chronically compare ourselves to others, we usually find ourselves at the short end of the stick. We tend to see others' strengths and our weaknesses and we let the comparison stand, even though it leaves us feeling inadequate, without asking any other questions about the validity of our basic premises.

The following exercise will allow you to use the admirable qualities you see in others as a springboard to developing these same qualities in yourself.

Exercise

Step One: Pick one person you admire. Write that person's name here:

_____

Step Two: Make a list of five adjectives that describe this person (i.e., smart, educated, confident, talented, funny).

1. _____

2. _____

3. _____

4. _____

5. _____

Step Three: Write an action plan for developing each of these characteristics in yourself.

1. _____

   _____

2. _____

   _____

3. _____

   _____

4. _____

   _____

5. _____

   _____

Step Four: Take action on your action plan. Three action steps I can take this week:

1. _____

2. _____

3. _____

Example

Step One: Tom Hanks

Step Two: (his characteristics)

(1) Decisive (2) Humorous (3) Courageous (4) Friendly (5) Creates opportunities

Step Three: (My plan for developing these same characteristics):

1. **Decisive.** Today I will make one decision and stand by it. I will tell John I was upset that he didn't call me back until a week after he said he would. I will write five pages of my short story. I will buy a journal and write my thoughts for today.

2. **Humorous.** Today I will begin to develop my sense of humor. This week I will learn a joke and tell it to a friend. I will buy Jerry Seinfeld's book. I will rent a comedy movie.

3. **Courageous.** Today I will acknowledge moments in my life when I have been courageous. I was brave to start therapy and share my private stories. I was courageous when I went whitewater rafting. I was courageous when I quit my job for a more meaningful one.

4. **Friendly.** Today I will be friendlier to others. I will smile and say hello to three new people as I walk down the street. I will call some friends and ask them how they are doing. I will affirm to myself "what goes around comes around."

5. **Create opportunities.** Today I will realize that I am the author of my life. I will make a list of five things I want to do but am avoiding. I will commit to doing one thing on this list today. I will tell one friend about my plans to be proactive and ask them to support me by holding me accountable.

Why People Might Admire You

In our experience, people caught in the trap of comparison thinking often feel that there's little to be admired in them, regardless of evidence to the contrary. If you truly feel you aren't admirable, perhaps it's because you've spent much of your life focused on other people's accomplishments.

The following exercise will help you to move your focus from comparison thinking back where it belongs—on your own self-assessment.

Exercise

List five reasons why someone would want you as a friend.

1. _____

2. _____

3. _____

4. _____

5. _____

List five reasons someone would want you as a boss.

1. _____

2. _____

3. _____

4. _____

5. _____

List five reasons someone would want you as a lover.

1. _____

2. _____

3. _____

4. _____

5. _____

List five reasons someone would want you as a sister or brother.

1. _____

2. _____

3. _____

4. _____

5. _____

Reclaiming Lost Parts of Your Personality

Even a happy life cannot be without a measure of darkness, and the word "happiness" would lose it's meaning if it were not balanced by sadness.

—Carl Jung

When we truly accept ourselves we may still compare ourselves to others. But our comparisons with others become more about what we have *in common* with them because we want to connect. When we are shaky in our sense of self, our comparisons are about how we are different and what we feel we must protect.

Self-acceptance means acknowledging and accepting the totality of our life experience. This includes not only our strengths and shining moments, but also accepting our struggles. It means making peace with our childhood hurts, losses, and shortcomings. It means accepting ourselves as imperfect human beings who make mistakes.

If we grew up in an environment with conditional love and rigid rules of expression, we learned (on a subconscious level) to disown many of our needs and those feelings that are not readily accepted by others. Carl Jung in many of his writings referred to this dark side of our experience as the "shadow." These are the parts of ourselves that we cannot bear to look at.

To accept our dark sides, we must first open ourselves to their existence. The following exercise will help you shine some light on the hidden parts of your personality.

I'm as pure as the driven slush.

—Tallulah Bankhead

Exercise: Accepting Your Shadow Self

Fill in the following chart. On one side write the qualities you will call "me." Now write as many characteristics that are typical of you as come to mind. On the other side of the centerline write the *opposite* qualities (e.g., the opposite of "giving" may be "self-absorbed," the opposite of "friendly" may be "reserved").

You will find that many of the opposite qualities will represent your disowned or the "shadow" parts of your personality. Your goal in this exercise is to identify and accept the truth of your shadow self.

It is important to understand that when we accept *all* the different parts of ourselves—without shame or judgment—we become more whole, less defensive, and, paradoxically, more capable of changing the shadow qualities. Accepting our "negative" traits does not mean we become "bad" people. As a rule, there are no moral issues involved. Our negative traits are generally solutions we created to meet unmet needs in childhood. They once helped us to survive but they no longer function as solutions and, in fact, may be blocking our growth as adults.

In this exercise you will try on these shadow traits as if they were articles of clothing. You will ask yourself, "In what ways does this characteristic apply to me?"

Example

Here's how one of our clients did this exercise:

Me (My Qualities)	Opposites (Shadow Self's Qualities)
1. Caring	1. Insensitive
2. Intelligent	2. Slow learner
3. Good athlete	3. Uncoordinated

4. Friendly	4. Rude
5. Organized	5. Spacey
6. Careful	6. Careless
7. Mellow	7. Hyper
8. Sincere	8. Manipulative
9. Punctual	9. Unreliable
10. Interesting	10. Boring

Now it's your turn.

Me (My Qualities)	Opposites (Shadow Self's Qualities)
1.	1.
2.	2.
3.	3.
4.	4.
5.	5.
6.	6.
7.	7.
8.	8.
9.	9.
10.	10.

It is very important to accept and own our shadow selves because if we are unable or unwilling to see the "opposite" qualities in ourselves, inevitably we will project them onto the outside world. For example, if we disown our anger, we most likely will experience the world as an angry place. If we disown caring, loving qualities, we will experience the world as loveless.

We learn as much from sorrow as from joy, as much from illness as from health, from handicap as from advantage—and indeed perhaps more.

—Pearl S. Buck

Exercise: Illuminating Your Blind Spots

This exercise is based on Gestalt therapy, which is a type of therapy that encourages the acceptance and ownership of all parts of the self. Doing the steps will help you learn to use the world as a mirror for reclaiming the missing or disowned parts of your identity.

1. Place your attention on an object in the room in which you are sitting.

2. Begin listing adjectives that describes this object in detail.

3. Now, take these adjectives and add them to the phrase "I am" (as shown in the examples below).

Do you notice any resistance to accepting these traits? Gently probe yourself and ask if there is any truth to this.

Example 1

1. A wood table

2. It is strong, graceful, supportive, has hard edges, is polished and artistic.

3. I am:

- I am strong   (I can accept that.)

- I am graceful   (I never thought of myself that way ... but I guess at times I am graceful.)

- I am supportive   (Yes.)

- I have hard edges   (Doesn't sound so good ... but I guess there is some truth to that.)

- I am polished   (I present myself that way a lot of times.)

- I am artistic   (I have trouble admitting this.)

Example 2

1. A flower

2. It is beautiful, graceful, delicate, intricate, and colorful.

3. I am:

- I am beautiful   (It's hard to admit.)

- I am graceful   (I never thought of that, but maybe at times.)

- I am intricate   (Yes.)

- I am colorful   (Interesting word, but I guess so.)

Now it's your turn. Try these for starters. Notice any resistance that comes up in accepting these qualities.

1. A skyscraper

2. A tree

3. A cat

4. A condemned building

5. The sun

Adjective	Your Ability to Accept This Part of Yourself
1.	
2.	
3.	
4.	
5.	

Now that you have some greater understanding of what is stopping you from approaching parts of your personality, it is time to begin expanding and clarifying your sense of self.

Getting Feedback

Knowing others is wisdom. Knowing the self is enlightenment.

—Lao-tzu

You may have found the last exercise quite difficult to do. Perhaps you are unable to tap that part of yourself that can identify your strengths. This may be because your family may have been unable to reflect back to you a clear picture of who you are. This process, as mentioned earlier, is called "mirroring." Mirroring is a vital process for the integration

of identity. If you didn't receive much mirroring from your family, it's not too late to receive mirroring from others.

Bill, a client, joined one of our therapy groups a few months after being seen on an individual basis. We believed a group would be an excellent environment for him to interact with others and receive some important feedback about how other people perceived him.

From the beginning Bill was well liked by all because of his wonderful sense of humor, his intelligence, and his instinctive skills for taking care of others. He was usually the first to provide support, insight, and a warm smile. So why was Bill even in therapy?

When asked to describe his childhood Bill painted a picture filled with details of a painful struggle with a learning disability, deep feelings of inadequacy, and an invalidating and conflictual family. Yet when he described these events, his face showed little or no expression, his voice was mild and even, and the only feeling he conveyed to the others in the group was one of a mild depression.

Over time, many feelings were mirrored back to Bill. As he described his father's insensitivity, the group suggested that he sounded angry. When he reported how a romance had failed, one member said to him, "You look sad," even though Bill had not said that he was sad. He was told that when matters become too intimate, too emotional, he makes jokes to lighten things up. His "caretaking" behavior was pointed out to him countless times.

This type of feedback, "mirroring," was new to Bill. His caretaking behavior was a survival strategy left over from his childhood. It had begun as an unconscious strategy to create a safety zone for himself. His jokes had been the way to diffuse conflict or to charm others. They also worked to derail intimacy.

His current detachment from his feelings was his childhood solution to a family that had no skills for handling pain, anger, or sorrow. It had helped him defuse the conflict in his family, but it had long since served its function; in his adult life it was preventing him from being able to sustain an intimate relationship.

This kind of mirroring made Bill aware of his blind spots and how they were affecting his relationships and his self-esteem. He then made it his goal to (1) practice tuning into his emotions and (2) to share his feelings more honestly with other people, both in and out of the group. Eventually, he reduced his caretaking behavior and began identifying and asserting his own needs. He still tells jokes from time to time, but now he is acutely aware of when they are used as distractions to keep himself and others from feeling emotional intimacy. He knows that if he is to meet his current goal—the development of his own identity—he will have to allow himself to feel the entire range of human emotions.

Exercise: Ask a Friend for Feedback about Yourself

Choose a supportive friend whom you trust enough to give you accurate feedback about yourself. Ask your friend to answer the following questions.

1. What do you see as my strengths?

2. What are areas you think I need to develop in myself?

3. When do you feel the closest to me?

4. Do I distance people? If so, how?

5. What do you think I could do to make my life more fulfilling?

Your Personal Rights

Part of developing your identity is practicing thoughts and phrases that affirm your personal rights. The following questionnaire will help you assess which of your personal rights need strengthening. Begin by taking the quiz below. Using a scale of one to ten, rate how true each statement is for you. For example, the first statement reads, "I have the right to say no to requests I do not want to meet." If you firmly believe this, rate it ten. A score of one would mean the statement is never true for you.

Your Personal Right	How Much You Believe This (1–10)
1. I have the right to say no to requests I do not want to meet.	
2. I have the right to ask for what I want.	
3. I have the right to have and express my feelings.	
4. I have the right to make mistakes.	
5. I have the right to be happy.	
6. I have the right to be listened to and understood.	
7. I have the right to follow my own decisions even if they differ from my family and friends.	
8. I have the right to change my mind.	
9. I have the right to be playful.	
10. I have the right to not be responsible for others.	
11. I have the right to grow.	
12. I have the right to live where I want.	
13. I have the right to choose work that makes me happy.	
14. I have the right to express my creative voice.	
15. I have the right to say "I don't know."	

16. I have the right to leave abusive people.	
17. I have the right to be angry with people I love.	
18. I have the right to make a lot of money.	
19. I have the right to my own personal space and time.	
20. I have the right to a loving, nurturing relationship.	

Scoring

Look over your scores. Any statement that you rate less than a seven can become one of your daily affirmations. Simply repeat it to yourself several times a day. Soon, you may find that you believe it. Additional positive affirmations will be found in the next section.

New Thoughts and Actions

> *Always be a first-rate version of yourself, instead of a second-rate version of somebody else.*
>
> —Judy Garland

Positive Affirmations You Can Say to Yourself

- I have talents and gifts unlike anyone else.

- I am not alone but part of something greater.

- I have a strong intuition, which connects me with truth and guidance that I can trust.

- I accept myself as I am.

- My wants and needs are important. I have a right to express them.

- As I embrace my "dark" qualities I learn the art of self-acceptance, bringing light to my life.

- I am a unique individual. I have a lot to offer this world.

- Beneath our masks, we are all children of God.

- Today I will accept my feelings and use them as a compass toward greater self-understanding and truth.

- Today I will stop looking for other people to tell me I am enough.

Positive Acts You Can Do for Yourself

- Write down five things you need from a friend and ask for them.

- Listen to motivational tapes and read inspiring books each day to continue your personal growth and build your self-esteem.

- Make notes in your journal to help clarify your feelings, wants, and reactions to others.

- Find a support group where you can express yourself more fully.

- Ask a trusted friend for feedback on your strengths and weaknesses.

- Stop isolating find people with common interests and share your thoughts.

- Start listening to your intuition.

- Begin listening to your heart for your true vision in life.

- Have the courage to admit when you are wrong and move on from there.

- Spend more time doing the things you love to do.

5

When You Can't Achieve the Success You Desire

The Fourth Key: Competence—Strengthening Your Confidence and Conquering Self-Sabotage

Understanding the Key Issue

Jeff, forty-three, a musician and songwriter, has invested nearly every bit of his savings in a home recording studio over the last ten years. It's become an amazing collection of high-tech equipment designed for creating state-of-the-art recordings. His goal is to record

demos of his original songs. He says, "I've been told I have a shot at selling a couple of my songs to a major artist. But these days you need the right equipment to produce a demo that will get them interested."

The trouble is, there seems to be no end to the equipment Jeff thinks he needs to get his demos to the point where he will be comfortable sending them out into the world. "Competition's fierce," he explains. His wife sees it differently. She says, "He's always tinkering in the studio. He can organize cables or make shelving units for his cassettes for hours. He can sit at his synthesizer spending hours just tweaking one sound."

Is Jeff a perfectionist? His wife doesn't think so. "I think he doesn't really want to finish his demo. He has songs that were 'finished' over five years ago that were never sent out. Others have been 'in the works' for years. Whenever something gets close to being finished, he buys a new piece of equipment and starts all over again. I doubt that he'll ever send a demo out to anyone."

An offhand remark from a friend was the start of Jennifer's inspiration for a business of her own. She was passing through the men's department at Bloomingdale's when she spotted a man she worked with who was frantically rummaging through a rack of ties. "Help me out, will you?" he said, waving her over. "You have good taste. You must be good at picking out ties."

Fifteen minutes later, purchases in hand, he grinned at her and said, "I should give you a commission."

His remark stayed in her mind. She knew so many men, busy executives who didn't have the time or the talent to shop for themselves. Her job as a lease manager for a real estate management firm was strictly dead-end. Perhaps here was a way to really make some money, doing something fun.

For a week the idea of having her own business as a personal shopper was an obsession. She thought of names, contacts, logos, business cards and spent her evenings drafting ads. She was almost ready to make the big move when something happened.

"I can't really explain it, but one day I was so excited, and the next day I thought the whole idea was stupid. I was supposed to meet with a career counselor to help design a business plan, but the night before the meeting I went out drinking with my friends. I was so hung over in the morning, I canceled the appointment. I lay in bed lecturing myself. While I didn't exactly love my job, it was a job—a steady income. I reminded myself that ninety percent of new businesses fail their first year. I thought that maybe what I really needed to do was go back to school to get my MBA."

Three years later, Jennifer has that MBA. She's also deeply depressed. "I can barely drag myself out of bed in the morning. I haven't circulated my resume. I feel as if I've climbed up some ladder that was standing against the wrong wall."

Does this sound strange? But how many of us have been close to achieving our goal, and then jumped off in some other direction? How many times have we said: *They'll never take someone with my lack of experience. . . . These poems are worthless, they just aren't finished yet. . . . I'd never qualify for a loan, so why bother? . . . I want to write a business plan, but I just don't have the time.*

When you have a hundred pages of notes that won't become a book, a ready-to-send resume that never gets mailed, a solid record at work that gets overlooked or minimized at promotion times, or a pile of top-of-the-line sporting equipment in your closet that

never gets used, it's time to take a hard look at what's preventing you from moving forward. What is it about those moments when we go from enthusiastic plans for success to a procrastination mode of avoidance and the mantra, "What's the use?"

Discovering the Roots of Your Struggle

*Everyone has talent. What is rare is the courage to follow
the talent to the dark place where it leads.*

—Erica Jong

Many teachers can tell you by second grade which children in their class are self-motivated and which are the yawners, procrastinators, and daydreamers. Think about that for a moment. By eight years old, some of us are already struggling to stay on task. What causes this? Although there may be no direct cause and effect, there are two types of situations that appear to sap motivation early on. These are (1) *overparenting*, or having parents who literally control their children, orchestrate their lives, and see them as extensions of themselves, and (2) *underparenting*, or having parents who neglect, abuse, or are indifferent to their children, coupled with few role models to help the children create a better dream for themselves. Let's look at these issues now.

Overparenting: Can a Parent Love Too Much?

*The proverb warns that "You should not bite the hand that feeds you."
But maybe you should, if it prevents you from feeding yourself.*

—Thomas Szasz

Brett, thirty-two, remembers, "My parents used to say, 'You can do anything you set your mind to, if you just try harder.' I had every kind of lesson a kid could have—golf, tennis, gymnastics—you name it. And it nearly killed my mother that I didn't excel in anything. I know she thought, 'We give you all of these things and all of these experiences, the least you can do in return is become a star at something.' I was always just average at everything I tried.

"Today I manage a department store and I guess you'd call me a moderate success. But to me, average means I've failed. People tell me, 'If you're unhappy there, quit the job and move on.' But there's this inertia I can't overcome."

Brett's parents meant to motivate, guide, and help him discover his talents. The trouble wasn't too little love and support, but too much. Afraid to try to be a "star" and to fail once again, he stayed stuck in a career he'd long ago outgrown.

Can you love a child too much? It depends on how you show this love. If you help a child learn and grow by balancing direction and discipline with a willingness at times to let go, you are on the right track. However, in your enthusiasm to be a good parent it's easy to fall into the trap of overparenting. In our book *When Parents Love Too Much* (1997) we drew distinctions between love and loving too much based on hundreds of interviews with parents and with adult children:

- Parents who love give time, attention, and affection to their children and provide for their emotional and physical needs. Parents who love too much become enmeshed in their children's daily lives and see their children as extensions of themselves.

- Parents who love are determined to be the best parents they can be, while recognizing that it's impossible to be perfect. Parents who love too much "overparent" and overprotect their children in an effort to dispel their own anxiety about being "good" parents, or to make up for their own childhood deprivations.

- Parents who love encourage independence and growth while setting appropriate limits, thus providing a safe environment for their children to explore and promoting their autonomy. Parents who love too much discourage their children's independence, seek to control their children's thoughts and actions, and unconsciously wish to mold their children into the image of their highest expectations of themselves.

On the positive side, children who were overparented often have a strong sense of belonging. Luanne recalls dating a man who took her to a party to which he wasn't invited. She cringed with embarrassment while he remained calm. "I don't care if I was invited or not," he told her. "I know these people and I belong here." On the negative side, however, they may have little experience with depending on themselves. They just aren't given enough time to experience trusting their own instincts before an overzealous parent steps in with advice and help. The fact that many of these parents are extremely accomplished and successful makes it understandable why their voices are difficult to ignore.

As a result, many children growing up with parents who "love too much" develop feelings of inadequacy when it comes to heeding their own voices. Sometimes, like Jeff, they become lost in their process and never get to the finished products of their work.

Sometimes, like Brett, they can't accept their limitations. Often they feel shut down at the starting line. As one woman put it, "It's a lot easier to say, 'I've failed because I didn't try,' than to say, 'I tried and I failed.'"

But the feeling that one should try to be a star is always there. Marianne Williamson, author of *A Return to Love* (1992), says that the reason so many of us are obsessed with becoming stars is that we're not yet starring in our own lives. Competence in childhood grows into adult self-confidence. But being rescued by parents or controlled by them leaves grown children with few inner resources for dealing with frustration. The result can be many dreams, many good ideas, and a lack of any follow-through energy or commitment.

Were You Overparented?

How many of the following statements do you agree with? Place a checkmark next to the ones that you relate to.

Too much attention was focused on me in childhood.	
I received an allowance well into adulthood (i.e., my parents paid my rent, gave me money each month, I had a trust fund, etc. .	
My parents have bailed me out more than once when I got into trouble.	
My parents took my side no matter what the specific circumstances of any conflict were, even though behind closed doors they might have said they were disappointed in me to each other.	
I often felt smothered by a parent's needs and requests.	
I have a pervasive sense of guilt when things don't go perfectly, even when I am not responsible.	
My parents did much of my homework if I appeared anxious, or they hired a succession of tutors.	
I have trouble making decisions, especially when I know my parents wouldn't approve.	
I feel guilty when I feel angry with my parents.	
I am very upset when I get criticized and I crave approval from others.	

The more statements you identify with, the more likely it is that you experienced some form of overparenting in childhood. While such a level of involvement with our parents can give us the assurance that someone cares deeply about us, it can also wreak havoc on our self-motivation. Brett identified with many of these statements. People like Brett feel ambivalent about success. On the one hand, they desire it deeply. On the other, they resent the notion that they have to "perform" to be accepted. Overparenting guarantees a lot of attention, but that attention comes with strings attached: "We've given you so much. Why aren't you *this*? Why aren't you *that*?"

Unfortunately, overparenting leads to self-doubt much more than to self-approval because our parents tend to overinflate our image of ourselves and then they encourage dependency on them at the same time. The root of procrastination is self-doubt. Imagine the self-doubt that ensues when your parents constantly tell you that you can do anything if you try hard enough, but then they say, "Not like that darling. Oh, no, start over again and do it just as I do." When Brett confronted his past honestly, he realized that the issues

of his childhood were being replayed in his thirties. Here is how he identified his current work-related issues:

Issue	Example
1. I have trouble taking the ball and running with it. **(Dependency)**	I tend to go to my boss with too many questions.
2. I can't get started. **(Procrastination)**	I often put off starting a project until the last minute.
3. I often break company rules when I think I won't get caught. **(Lack of responsibility; feeling entitled to stretch the rules)**	I'm late. I tend to call in sick (e.g., fellow workers need to reschedule meetings to more convenient times for me).
4. I've been told that I'm too quiet during meetings. **(Nonparticipation)**	I find it difficult to express myself in a work environment.
5. I'm not sure I have the energy to put in the time my boss does. After all, why should I get on a plane once a week for 60K a year? **(Ambivalence about success)**	I feel both good and bad when I get a decent year-end review. I feel good that my work has been noticed. I resent the notion that now I'm expected to do even better in the next year.
6. My co-workers sometimes do my share. I pay them back by taking them to dinner or letting them borrow my parent's condo at Vail to go skiing. **(Attracting rescuers)**	I am good at manipulating others to take care of me by pouting or looking depressed. I only doubt myself later, after I've gotten what I wanted.

Now it's your turn. Fill in the following chart with the issues and examples that feel true for you.

Issue	Example
1. Dependency:	

2. Procrastination:	
3. Responsibility:	
4. Non-participation:	
5. Ambivalence about success:	
6. Attracting rescuers:	

If you want a place in the sun, you must leave the shade of the family tree.

—Osage saying

Were You Underparented?

Nothing has stronger influence psychologically on their environment,
and especially on their children, than the unlived lives of the parents.

—Carl Jung

The child who was neglected, physically and/or psychologically abused, or basically ignored may feel that he or she has little in common with those who were overparented and had so much provided for them on the proverbial silver platter. But underparenting is the flip side of the same coin.

You may also have childhood needs that were never met appropriately which continue to affect you as an adult. You, too, may feel stuck at the starting line, but for many different reasons: death, divorce, illness, abuse, and neglect can all create situations in families where children's needs go unmet. As one client, Sandra, put it, "My father died in a plane crash when I was twelve and there's been a lot of bitterness in my life because of it. I didn't grow up the way other kids did. I had it hard. There's a part of me that thinks, 'Shouldn't it finally equal out for me? Doesn't life owe me something?'"

Sandra was a very hard worker who had graduated from a Big Ten university. Her first year at any job was always met with excellent reviews. Then, she'd begin miss deadlines. For example, a memo that was supposed to be prepared, approved, and sent out for review by Tuesday morning would not be completed until Wednesday afternoon when she would finally finish writing it. The memo would be terrific, but after its obligatory review by her superiors, it arrived on the desks of those who needed it too late to be useful.

Sandra's pattern also played out in her relationships with men. During her first year in a relationship she would be happy and content. But at the end of a year the relationship would collapse. Recently, while dining with her boyfriend at a good restaurant to celebrate their first anniversary, she began undermining and criticizing him. Then she apologized for her ill-tempered remarks with a wounded look as she pushed an expensive meal around on her plate because she just didn't feel hungry.

Given Sandra's history, her actions made sense. At the deepest level, underparented children want to know that they are accepted and loved without having to demonstrate the hard work, achievement, or self-sacrifice that were their safety nets during their very rocky childhood. As adults, they may think, "For what I've been able to achieve in spite of my awful childhood, don't I deserve something extra now?" They often test people and situations to see if they can win unconditional acceptance and sabotage themselves at the same time.

Both the underparented child and the overparented child can end up with some behaviors in common that stand in the way of the success they desire. That is, they may share a feeling of entitlement and a proclivity toward feelings of demand-resistance (chronic negativity) and/or abandonment depression. We'll explore these terms in greater depth in the sections that follow.

Do You Suffer from Feelings of Entitlement?

Nancy panicked as she raced out of the meeting. The note her assistant had handed her was ominous: "It's Michael. He's calling from his car phone. I told him you were in a meeting, but he said to interrupt. It's an emergency." It could only mean one thing. Someone was dead.

"Mike?!" Nancy wheezed into the phone. "Are you okay?"

"Sure, babe. But I can't find the garage door opener. I'm parked in the alley. Do you know where it is?"

Nancy knew where it was, all right. It was hanging on the visor, about four inches from his face. She took a deep breath, told him where to look, and thought to herself, "This is a man who graduated from a prestigious university, but he can't locate the aspirin or his car keys without enlisting my help. He wanders off to the beach while I type his memos, and then he criticizes me for being so serious all the time."

People like Michael possess what therapists call a deep sense of psychological entitlement—unconscious, projected expectations that the world will pay special attention to them, anticipate their needs, and rescue them when they need help. The root of such expectations lies in childhood. From the time of their birth, many people became the center of their parents' lives. Freud referred to this phenomenon as "His Majesty the Baby."

In this type of family, all a child has to do to get his/her needs met is to pretend to be helpless.

A sense of entitlement is the expectation that the world will automatically treat us well, it will rescue us, provide for us and appreciate us. You might be wondering: What's so bad about feeling entitled? Wouldn't it be worse to feel undeserving? Perhaps. But entitlement feelings often lead to passive behaviors. For example, "If she doesn't have the time to pick up the phone and call me, I'm not going to call her." Or, "He should know what I want for my birthday. I shouldn't have to hint around." And, "I'm not going to write thank-you letters for job interviews. They should thank me for taking the afternoon off and coming in." Or even, "Take extra courses in my spare time at my own expense? No way. If the company wants me to get more training, they should pay for it."

Joan, for example, was told that she needed to contribute more to department meetings. "I got so angry. These people in my department go on and on and you can't get a word in edgewise. My boss takes no control over the meeting to see that everyone gets a chance to speak. My feeling is, if they aren't willing to shut up and listen, why should I bother?"

When Joan was growing up, her sisters and brothers monopolized the discussion at the dinner table. But Joan's mother would step in and say, "Now let's listen to what Joan did today. Joan? Come on, honey. How was school?" And then she'd ask Joan a lot of questions until Joan would finally answer, and in a moment of great satisfaction she knew that everyone was listening to what she had to say.

The Entitlement Quiz

You might not think of yourself as having entitlement issues because the word "entitled" has so many negative connotations. But the sense of psychological entitlement is often unconscious. It appears in our actions, not necessarily in our thoughts.

In the following quiz, assign a number that best describes how you feel concerning each of the following questions. Base your answers on what has been true for you for *the greater part of your life*. The best answer is usually what most quickly comes to your mind.

The scale is:

Strongly Disagree	Mildly Disagree	Neutral	Mildly Agree	Strongly Agree
0	1	2	3	4

1. When people tell me their problems I wait for the moment to take center stage and tell about a problem of mine.	
2. I have left tasks unfinished, believing that others will complete them.	
3. I've played "poor" and expected others to pick up the tab, especially when I knew someone's salary was more than mine.	
4. I don't do everyday tasks of cleaning, washing the dishes, or paying the bills. I have other people who take care of such tasks.	

5. I get angry when people make requests of me. I feel they are infringing on my spare time.	
6. When I need the answer to a question or help with something that needs doing, I can get really angry when the person I ask to help me won't stop what he or she is doing and listen to me.	
7. I pout or look sad when people don't listen to me.	
8. I'm late for many things in life, but I never thought of tardiness as such a big deal.	
9. I grab the best seat in movies, airplanes, or at restaurants without asking others what they might want. I get claustrophobic without my "space."	
10. I have borrowed things and forgotten to return them.	

Scoring

Scores of 25 and above are frequently found among people who have some degree of entitlement issues. If you scored 25 or more, ask yourself to what degree your expectations of others may be contributing to feelings of disappointment, frustration, and even depression. Sometimes, just knowing that feelings of entitlement exist is enough to challenge old patterns of thinking and to create change in your life.

Demand-Resistance

If you find you can't move forward toward your goals, you may suffer from demand-resistance in addition to an unconscious sense of entitlement. Demand-resistance is a chronic negative response to obligations or expectations. It is almost always unconscious. For example, if you make daily lists of things to do, which you seldom complete, you are being demand-resistant. Or you understand that you're the only one who will suffer if you don't take your car in to be serviced, but still you resent doing it and never quite find time for it. These kinds of things occur because you hate being told what to do, even when you're the one giving the orders.

Controlling parents and teachers encourage and foster demand-resistance: "Take out the dog, now. And clean your room, right after you take out the dog." But hours later, "Didn't you hear me? The dog is peeing on the rug!" Play this game often enough, and you won't be elected for this particular job anymore.

Demand-resistance has its payoffs. By withholding what another requests of you, you assert your power. Then, the other may stop making the demands on you and do things for you. You can also avoid doing things you're afraid to do, on principle, and avoid coming face to face with possible failure. In addition you avoid having to engage in more active types of conflict, such as bluntly saying, "No, I won't do it."

"My sister's like that!" one client told us. "When my mother issues orders like the commandant she is, I argue with her. My sister just says, 'Sure, Mom. Okay, Mom.' But she never does what she promises she'll do, and it doesn't even bother her."

The costs of demand-resistance can be tremendous, however. Activities you enjoy, such as playing tennis or jewelry making, must be performed outstandingly or given up completely. You may find yourself setting goals and then sabotaging them, making demands of yourself and resisting them. You may even get angry with yourself, but you can't break the pattern.

There is a solution, however. The more sure you are of yourself, the more you work on building a strong sense of who you are, the less vulnerable you'll feel to the possibility of being run over by someone else, and the less likely you will be to resist meeting your own goals—just to prove a point.

Exercise: Are You Demand-Resistant?

Place a checkmark next to the statements that apply to you.

1. When you were younger, did you procrastinate or "resist" finishing school homework assignments?	
2. Did your parents tell you what to do and how to do it constantly?	
3. When someone asks you to do something, do you feel tense or resentful?	
4. Do you have trouble with authority figures?	
5. Do you have difficulty finishing tasks that are asked of you?	
6. Do you make to-do lists and then never look at them?	

If you answered yes to two or more of the proceeding questions, there is an excellent chance that you have aspects of demand-resistance. It is important to understand that you may habitually perceive *all* tasks as demands. It is also important to realize that your resistance places you in a reactive rather than proactive position with life. To create the success you want in life, it is essential that you disarm your demand-resistance, so you can move freely toward achieving the goals you set for yourself.

Abandonment Depression and the Fear of Being Yourself

What is *abandonment depression*? When many people begin to pursue their goals, the necessity of asserting themselves, or of translating their deepest desires into action fills them with a sense of panic. Someone pursuing a cherished dream, especially one that requires risk taking, must assert him- or herself: "This is who I am, this is what I want, this is what I deserve." The trouble is, many people have never had any support for taking such stands and, consequently, they struggle with a lack of faith in their own beliefs. As a rule, when they were children, they received the following types of feedback when they tried to assert themselves:

"Don't think what you think, feel what you feel, or do what you want to do."

Expressing yourself may have resulted in the loss of love or approval from your parents or friends. Your unique characteristics weren't defined, mirrored, or acknowledged. As a result, you may have developed what therapists refer to as a "false self" in order to ward off emotional abandonment.

To avoid the fear and the depression that resulted when your real self emerged, a false self may have been created to restructure life and make it feel "safer." The unconscious thought was: "I'll give up searching for my real self and all that would make me truly happy in exchange for never feeling the fear of being alone or the pain of abandonment."

Insensitive teachers and counselors can also squelch your confidence and drive. One of our clients, forty-one-year-old Mary, recalls wanting to enroll in college a year early through a special early admissions program that allowed promising high school juniors to skip their senior years. "But my high school counselor said, 'Sorry I can't write a recommendation for you. I don't believe in these programs.'" Many of her fellow classmates withdrew their applications. Mary was about to do the same when a cousin told her, "Look, maybe your counselor is jealous. After all, he had to do the full four years." Mary persevered until she found an understanding French teacher who wrote the needed recommendation, and she enrolled early and did well.

Your husband, children, and/or your friends may be quick to point out reasons why you will never realize your dreams. This kind of discouragement can also lead to abandonment depression—the land called "Why Bother?"

"You can't do it alone; you need me to do it for you."

In the past, it may have been as subtle as having your parents do your homework the moment you became frustrated, or constantly reminding you of all the chores that you needed to do . Today, it may be a lover or spouse undermining you and making you feel that you can't think independently or act successfully alone. Such messages add up to ambivalence about success. And, by its very nature, ambivalence about a goal can wreck your chances for achieving it.

Self-Sabotage: The Hidden Payoffs

Many clients have reported that, when they begin thinking about making real changes in their lives, a period of acting out results. They go on drinking binges, overeat, overspend, oversleep, gamble, and become sexually promiscuous. These types of self-destructive behavior are actually attempts to avoid feeling depressed or worthless.

Karl, for example, had the idea of supplementing his income by giving computer lessons. He put an ad in the neighborhood paper promising a brochure of his services, free to callers. He received ten calls. He sat down to write his brochure and suddenly the words just wouldn't come. He spent hours at his computer, exploring websites, chatting in online forums. Two weeks passed, and, by then, he figured the callers would have forgotten about their need for his services anyway—so why write the brochure?

All self-defeating behavior has a hidden function. Originally, most of our current problems were protective solutions to early life struggles. When we felt threatened—physically or emotionally—we adapted our behavior to create *safety* even if it sabotaged

our ability to express ourselves or to find happiness. Let's look at some of the hidden payoffs that underlie self-defeating behavior:

- You feel more secure because when you hide your talents, no one can criticize you for not doing spectacularly well.

- You are "paying back" someone else—"getting even." For example, not finishing your college degree could be a payback for your parents who always pushed you to perform.

- You don't really want to meet your stated goal—you just want to prove yourself to someone else. When that person doesn't pay you any attention or give you the admiration you seek, you jettison your plan.

Self-defeating behavior is habit-forming. Each time you give up you reinforce this pattern.

How do you "act out" or avoid following through on your goals? Place a checkmark next to the activities that apply to you.

Avoidance or Acting Out Behavior	
I spend hours watching mindless TV.	
I drink too much.	
I shop too much.	
I gamble.	
I oversleep.	
I smoke pot or do hard drugs.	
I become promiscuous.	
I putter around.	
I get depressed.	
I go off on tangents.	
I start arguments.	
Other:	

Scoring

Now review the activities you've checked. Ask yourself if you have attempted to "pay back" someone or get even somehow through this behavior. Try to pinpoint exactly what it is you are avoiding—a person, a fear, or a feeling.

Realizing Why It Will Never Be Enough

"The idea didn't have merit. That's why I didn't follow through." So you say. But don't believe it. Brian Tracy once wrote, "The average person has four ideas a year which, if any one is acted on, would make him or her a millionaire."

We can't tell you what will happen if you pursue your goal or your dream. We can't assure you that you'll succeed, or predict that you'll fail. But, we can tell you exactly what will occur if you are the type of person who has many creative ideas and thoughts that you never fully pursue:

- You are likely to compromise your most significant talents or push aside your dreams to pursue something that seems more tangible and secure. But because the path you choose ensures you will never be able to express yourself fully, when you achieve some secondary goal you still will feel unfulfilled and stuck.

- You will spend much of your energy in wishful thinking. People often cling to the hope that something will happen to propel them out of their current situation without the need for them to take any real steps toward change. They believe that the "cure" has to come from the outside, since they feel ineffectual in making changes themselves. Years spent in this kind of wishful thinking end up with a person waking up one day thinking, "Why didn't I ever try? Why did I let so much pass me by?"

- You may become impulsive. The need to have a purpose coupled with the fear of self-exploration may lead to impulsivity. One client, for example, admitted that her obsession with having a baby didn't stem from a need to nurture. "I'll finally have something to say to people who keep asking me what I'm doing with my life." Too afraid to give her marriage a year or two of mutual exploration and getting to know each other, she got pregnant on her honeymoon.

- You keep digging in the ashes. Because you tend to focus on things and people outside yourself to make you happy, you blame the boss's nit-picking for your sense of frustration, or your wife's nagging for your unhappiness. You concentrate on getting other people and situations to change instead of on expressing your talents. You try to make the unsatisfactory satisfying by bending others to your will. It never quite happens. You still feel stuck.

RX: Building Up Your Feeling of Competence

We don't know who we are until we see what we can do.

—Martha Grimes

Your Key Questions

1. What do I need to change or develop in myself to become more successful?
   (E.g., *increase my stamina, perseverance, confidence, willingness to work my way up more slowly than I'd like.*)

_____

_____

_____

_____

_____

_____

2. What teachers or mentors can I find who will help me develop my interests or career?
   (E.g., *a career counselor, a successful friend, a high school teacher.*)

_____

_____

_____

_____

_____

_____

3. What is a description of a job that would bring me greater satisfaction?
   (E.g., *hours, location, level of responsibility, values, work atmosphere.*)

_____

_____

_____

_____

_____

_____

_____

4. What are three things that, if I did them consistently for the next month, would make a real difference in my path to greater success?
   (E.g., *set goals; get up earlier; stop defying authority.*)

_____

_____

_____

_____

_____

See How Your Symptoms Serve You

When we're all process and no product, we usually spend a lot of time berating ourselves. That's time that could be spent more pleasantly and productively. You may be missing opportunities, disregarding your greatest talents, and living on the periphery of life. Why hold on to such a pattern? Understanding how your symptoms seem to serve a positive purpose in your life is the first step in learning to manage procrastination, entitlement feelings, self-sabotage, and passivity.

Examples

Symptom	Protective Function
1. Procrastination	Provides a reason for failing that doesn't relate to your intelligence, skill, or competence.
2. Entitlement	Get others to take responsibility and cater to your needs.

3. Self-sabotage	Safety from risk or increased responsibility.
4. Passivity	Avoid risk, hoping to get needs met without having to ask.
5. Demand-resistance	Feeling in control, not pushed around.

Creating New Choices

- "I'm bored and restless most of the time. I feel like I'm spending my life waiting for something exciting to happen."

- "In some ways I feel like my life hasn't really started yet."

- "I know I could run my own business—a gift shop on the North Shore where people have money to burn. But I just can't discipline myself."

- "I've been saying I'll start my novel for the last three years now. I have half a page written."

Given your history, it's understandable that you might feel unconsciously ambivalent about success. There's a tremendous downside to the scenario we've been looking at in this chapter that has nothing to do with dollars and cents. All of the people who shared their stories in this chapter were out of touch with their talents. Behind their outward confidence was a fair amount of self-doubt. However, when they conquered self-doubt, they were able to unleash enormous amounts of pent-up energy. So can you. You begin by looking at each symptom, major or minor, that fuels your dissatisfaction with your life, and you can begin to create new choices.

Exercise: Finding New Solutions

- In the first column, write the symptoms you identified in "See How Your Symptoms Serve You."

- In the second column, write the original protective function of this strategy.

- In the third column, write the downside to this solution.

- In the fourth column, write a more effective solution to this problem.

Example

Symptom	Protective Function	Downside to This Solution	New Choices
Can't start my novel.	I don't have to find out that I'm not a great writer. I keep my dreams alive.	I don't find out whether I can write at all. Recycles self-criticism and feelings of inadequacy.	Write an outline. Write a description of the characters. Get support. Explore the reasons why I want to write.
I feel my life hasn't started. I'm not really clear about what I want to do with my life.	I can say I'm lazy instead of I tried and I failed. I can keep hoping some incredible opportunity will knock at my door. I can fantasize about becoming an overnight success.	I end up depressed and stressed out. I feel I'm letting my family down.	See a career counselor. List the things I've done in my life that I really enjoyed doing.

Now it's your turn.

Symptom	Protective Function	Downside to This Solution	New Choices
1.			
2.			
3.			

You Have a Unique Voice—Learn to Use It with Confidence

At bottom every man knows well enough that he is a unique being, only once on this earth: and by no extraordinary chance will such a marvelously picturesque piece of diversity in unity as he is, ever be put together a second time.

—Friedrich Wilhelm Nietzche

Many people who feel unsure of their own talents become masters at finding a complimentary person who is confident, goal-oriented, and willing to take on more than fifty percent of the responsibility for the relationship.

Jim, a thirty-five-year-old bartender, admits, "The last four relationships I've had, have been with highly competent women. My last girlfriend, Ellen, made over a hundred-thousand dollars a year. She would take us on extravagant vacations four times a year. I paid half the rent, but I know she paid ninety percent of our expenses. She said she didn't care, that we weren't about money.

"It was wonderful to have someone take of me that way, but on some level I always felt a sense of shame, like I was being a sponge. In therapy, it was pointed out to me that, in my childhood, my parents were always rescuing me when I was anxious or loading me up with money, even when I didn't ask for it. But the truth is I often got angry with them, just as I got angry at Ellen and criticized her and put her down. At times, I hurt her badly. It's not something I'm proud of. I'd like to do better next time."

Jim was a man who had lost his "voice." His opinions and thoughts about the next move, the next goal, were overlooked and ignored by others who always seemed to know better or be more confident than he was. Because he was afraid to fail, he listened to their voices, rather than his own. This was an enormous loss to his self-esteem. "I have tried very hard in the last two years to take on more responsibility. It has been difficult, but each time I complete a task all by myself it feels good."

At first, thinking for yourself without relying on the advice of others may trigger feelings of fear or inadequacy. Expect this. But you have a unique voice, your own special "take" on the world that is valuable. When your inner voice speaks to you, it can be very comfortable to reply, "Yes, but maybe I better ask my friend Anne what she thinks, or run this by my father." Other people can be helpful, but learning to trust your inner voice and acting on it can provide you with a level of satisfaction and confidence unlike anything else you have ever known.

How do you begin? First, you must take a hard look at the rescuers in your life and begin to ease yourself away from their advice and control.

Stop Attracting Rescuers

True self-esteem, a genuine sense of one's self as worthy of nurture and protection, capable of growth and development stems from the experience of competence . . . no one can give another the experience of competence: one must achieve that for oneself.

—Michael Franz Basch

Make no mistake about this. People love to give advice. Some will confidently steer you through your life while they completely neglect their own. And there are those super-competent individuals who thrive on helping everyone around them. Your task isn't to throw away good advice when you get it. It's to give your own voice a little more airtime. First, you have to look squarely at how much you rely on others for their blessing before you can feel confident in what you think and feel. Then, you're going to have to stop consulting "rescuers" and take a leap of faith in yourself.

For the next exercise, in the first column put together a list of five specific times you reeled in someone else to finish a task that you could have done for yourself, or you sought and took advice that you really didn't need.

In the second column, write out the action step that would have meant listening to and trusting your own voice.

Examples

Attracting Rescuers	Listening to My Own Voice
1. I looked overly anxious, so my boyfriend read the draft of my proposal and rewrote it.	1. Finish the assignment myself.
2. I let my father do my taxes when I was 33 years old. I was feeling overwhelmed by the whole process.	2. Realize I need to learn how to do my taxes myself, and set a goal to learn the basics while asking my father to teach me the fine points.
3. Left the bathroom a mess so that my wife would clean it up.	3. Make it a priority to keep a clean bathroom so that I can feel good about my surroundings and my ability to take charge.
4. Wanted to buy a time-share in the Caribbean, but got talked out of it by a friend.	4. Clarify what I really want, realize that what someone else sees as a waste of money reflects their goals and not necessarily mine.

Now it's your turn.

Attracting Rescuers	Listening to My Own Voice
1.	1.

2.	2.
3.	3.
4.	4.
5.	5.

Developing Self-Discipline

Discipline is remembering what you want.

—David Campbell

There are few personal traits that most of us wish we had more of than self-discipline. Most of us also have absolutely no idea how to accomplish that longed-for state.

A friend of ours, on a ten-city tour to promote his new book on school reform, found himself in a bookstore in Boston one stormy afternoon. He was surrounded by stacks of books waiting to be autographed, but there were no customers. It was time to pack up when two women finally walked up to his table. One opened his book and paged through it, then she turned to her friend and said, "Just look at this. I could have written this!" and she eyed our friend with barely concealed contempt. "I'll bet you're not teaching anymore. I'd write reams about school reform, too, if I wasn't so busy grading papers."

For the record, he teaches at an inner city school, grades hundreds of papers each term, trains student teachers, teaches an evening course, and spends time with his family. He is philosophic about such comments. "As a writer, you hear it all the time—'I could write this or I could write that,' or even, 'I have this great idea, why don't I tell it to you and you write it and I'll give you ten percent.' Sure, some of them could do it. The difference between me and them is I *can* do it, and I *do* do it."

His secret to getting his writing done? Self-discipline.

Goals and lists are supposed to be helpful guides and motivators. For some of us, however, it often works like this: "I should diet, I should write a resume, and I should

clean my desk. I hate this. It all feels like too much pressure. I think I'm out of cat food. I'll go to the store and come back to this later." But "later" never comes. By ignoring a goal or responsibility it feels as though we're finally standing up to some autocratic parent and saying, "I'll show you that you can't make me do this—*there!*"

If you tend to react to directions like a rebellious adolescent told to take the garbage out on a Saturday morning, substitute "I choose to" or "I want to" for "You should" or "I should." Remove the demand and you'll remove much of the resistance. Harping at yourself with disapproving words, or calling yourself lazy, sets up a cycle of anxious striving and pushing, which eventually leads to the resistance that ultimately defeats you.

Exercise: What Have I Accomplished?

For one week, keep track of what you've done, not what you should have done. Often when we take a good, hard look at what we're expecting ourselves to do, we realize no one could accomplish it, because our goals are contradictory or unreasonable.

	Sunday	Monday	Tuesday	Wednesday	Thursday	Friday	Saturday
1.							
2.							
3.							
4.							
5.							
6.							
7.							
8.							

Ambivalence

A second roadblock to self-discipline is ambivalence. This is the distinguishing characteristic of those who cannot get their dreams to get off the ground. They buy the latest diet books, the newest computer programs, and the latest ski technology. They spend top dollar to surround themselves with the finest equipment in hopes that it will motivate them. They study, study, study. But they don't diet, they don't compute, they don't exercise, and they don't pass go.

Perhaps you don't finish what you start because it's the finishing that's so frightening. As one man put it, "I would sit down at my desk to work on the proposal and then I'd see a streak on the window and I'd think, 'I should clean that.' I haven't thought of cleaning windows since I moved in here two years ago, but suddenly it became the most compelling thing I had to do." That afternoon he learned that he had enormous self-discipline. Only it was about cleaning windows. He used old newspaper to get the streaks out, working on them for hours. But he ultimately learned he had enormous ambivalence about his business proposal that was going to continue to lead to fears and paralysis until he dealt with it, one issue at a time.

The key questions for him turned out to be: "Do I really want it? Am I ready to move forward? If not, why not? Am I secretly afraid of discovering my true voice?"

Many of you fail to finish what you start because you have doubts about whether the end product will be worthwhile. What if, after all of this hard work, it isn't as wonderful as you imagined it would be? What then?

As strange as it may seem, dreams of perfection, fame, and glory are a third motivational drain. Our successful author friend admits that when he first started writing, all he could think about was having his work become a best-seller. He'd sit at his computer and daydream about seeing his name on the *New York Times* best-seller list, and his self-discipline would go out the window. "I think I had to constantly imagine myself as a star because I was doing battle with a voice inside that said, 'You're worthless, a failure, and who do you think you are to say you can write?' Now I just write, to write; to see something finished."

Self-discipline, then, isn't something we have or don't have like blue eyes or curly hair. It's something we build. It comes from the simple accumulation of positive experience, of doing what needs to be done, step by step, even though it may be frustrating, even though we may be afraid. We start working through the feelings, instead of trying to get away from them. In the end, the process builds strength and hope. That is what ultimately gives us the motivation to get up the next day and do it again.

So how can you do it? Doing the following exercises will give you some practice.

Make Your Goals Work for You

Goals are dreams with deadlines.

—Diana Scharf Hunt

Exercise: Create *SMART* Goals

SMART goals are *Sensible, Measurable, Achievable, Realistic,* and *Timebound.* Here are several examples:

Goal: I will send out my three-song demo tapes to three music publishers listed in the *Songwriters Marketplace.*

Sensible: Because I have a number of beautiful, marketable songs and I think other people would enjoy hearing them. Also, a well-known artist might become interested in singing one of these songs.

Measurable: I will finish the tape and cassette labels by March 15 of this year.

Achievable: I've been playing music and writing songs since I was fourteen. It's true the market is difficult to break into, but there are plenty of people who persevere and get their songs sold.

Realistic: I'm not expecting to hear from Madonna's people, or that Quincy Jones will discover my songwriting and change my life. I'm looking for feedback.

Timebound: I will find three appropriate publishers and place it in the mail by April 1 of this year.

Goal: To leave teaching and set up a private practice as a tutor.

Sensible: Tutors get $65 an hour, which is much more than the hourly rate I make in the public schools. I know teachers who will refer students to me.

Measurable: I will have five students within ninety days.

Achievable: There is a definite market for these services. I just need to get my name out there.

Realistic: I will have to tutor twenty hours a week to equal my salary. That's possible.

Timebound: If I take a year off from teaching and this doesn't work out, I can go back to the classroom.

Now it's your turn.

Goal: _____

_____

_____

Sensible: _____

_____

Measurable: _____

_____

_____

Achievable: _____

_____

_____

Realistic: _____

_____

_____

Timebound: _____

_____

_____

Goal: _____

_____

_____

Sensible: _____

_____

_____

Measurable: _____

_____

_____

Achievable: _____

_____

_____

Realistic: _____

_____

_____

Timebound: _____

_____

_____

Exercise: The Cost of Not Following Through

How can you stay motivated? Tony Robbins in *Awaken the Giant Within* has a simple recipe for staying motivated: "Everything you and I do, we do either out of our need to avoid *pain* or our desire to gain *pleasure*." In other words, people who procrastinate do it because they associate more pain with doing the task than pleasure with completing it. "If we link massive pain to any behavior or emotional pattern, we will avoid indulging in it at all costs. We can use this understanding to harness the force of pain and pleasure to change virtually anything in our lives" (1991, 55).

Now, write a paragraph on what the result would be if you don't follow through on the goals you wrote in the previous exercise.

_____

_____

_____

_____

_____

_____

_____

_____

Stop Yourself from Going off on Tangents

One of the ways we manage our anxiety about completing tasks is to shift our attention to something else. You may find an incredible urge to clean your car as you approach the deadline of your project. Or maybe you start tuning out in front of the Jerry Springer show to avoid doing your income taxes. You may rationalize the importance of these

distractions. "But the car is such a mess—cleaning it will be really good for my morale." "I really need to relax with the tube tonight; I'll do my taxes after I relax and build up some energy reserves."

One of the most important things you can learn to do is to begin your day with the tasks you are most likely to avoid.

Exercise: Create a Daily To-Do List for One Week That Shows the "Pain" and "Drain"

Example

Here's Karen's to-do list for Saturday:

1. Water garden

2. Call Lori and arrange to meet her for dinner

3. Call insurance companies for lower car insurance rate

4. Call Mom

5. Move winter clothes to the back of closet

6. Go grocery shopping

As with most to-do lists, when Karen first looked at it she realized she really didn't want to do any of it. This is why these kinds of tasks end up on a list. The things you want and love to do you don't usually need to write down and remind yourself about.

We advised Karen to look at her lists in terms of the pain and the drain. The pain is why she doesn't want to do it. The drain is what the results are going to be if she doesn't do it. Here's her list, rewritten with the most draining items first.

Karen's Revised To-Do List

Goal	Pain	Drain
1. Call Mom.	She's only going to complain about Dad, and I can't go to visit her over this weekend.	She'll keep calling and I'll keep feeling guilty. It's better to get a lecture at 9 am and be done with it than to dread it all day and then get the lecture anyway.
2. Move winter clothes to the back of the closet.	Boring, tedious.	I will spend another week being late for work because it takes me so long to find something to wear, because my closet is such a mess.

3. Call insurance companies for lower rates.	I hate this stuff.	I am wasting a thousand dollars a year.
4. Go grocery shopping.	Time-consuming and irritating.	There is nothing in the refrigerator and I am spending a fortune eating all my meals out.
5. Call Lori and arrange to meet her for dinner.	We'll argue when we are deciding on a restaurant.	Sitting home on a Saturday night.
6. Water garden.	It's the only thing I want to do!	I could spend all day in the garden and feel guilty about everything else I haven't done.

Responsibility means not blaming anyone or anything for your situation, including yourself. It is the ability to have a creative response to the situation as it is now.

—Depak Chopra

Building Your Support Team

Winners can tell you where they are going, what they plan to do along the way, and who will be sharing the adventure with them.

—Denis Waitley

Make a list of friends and colleagues who truly support your developing sense of competence. This means people who will help you stay on course without rescuing you. These are friends who know of your goals to develop your sense of power and to express your true voice in the world. You might develop a strategy to check in with them once a week to discuss your successes and your frustrations.

This support team should be mutual. Part of developing your own self-esteem is learning to support others on their paths. Your support team will gently monitor your dependency and victim tendencies while empowering solutions rather than intensifying problems.

Three friends who will support me in my personal growth:

1. _____

2. _____

3. _____

I promise to share my personal goals with at least one of these people this week.

Signed _____

Listen to Inspirational Speakers

The expectations of life depend upon diligence;
the mechanic who would perfect his work must first sharpen his tools.

—Confucius

Another terrific way to increase your motivation and rewrite your negative belief system is to listen to motivational speakers every day. Today, it is easier than ever to find books or tapes that you can buy, rent, or check out of the library that will inspire and energize you to reach your goals. You will set off instant bursts of energy as you listen to the success secrets and attitude of the masters. (See also the Resources and Suggested Reading sections at the back of this book for more suggestions.)

Suggested Books and Audio Tapes

Blanchard, Kenneth. 1993. *The One-Minute Manager*. Berkeley, CA: Berkeley Publishing Group.

Blanchard, Kenneth, and Spencer Johnson. 1982. *The One-Minute Manager*. New York: William Morrow.

Brown, Les. 1992. *Live Your Dreams*. San Francisco: Harper Audio (audiocassettes).

Canfield, Jack, and Mark Victor Hansen. 1996. *Dare to Win*. Berkeley: Berkeley Publishing Group.

Canfield, Jack. 1995. *Self-Esteem and Peak Performance*. Careertrack, Inc. (audiotape).

Covey, Stephan. 1989. *The Seven Habits of Highly Effective People*. New York: Simon & Schuster.

Dyer, Wayne. 1989. *You'll See It When You Believe It*. New York: Avon Books.

Hay, Louise. 1995. *101 Power Thoughts*. Carson, CA: Hay House (audiocassette).

Jeffreys, Michael. 1996. *Success Secrets of the Motivational Superstars*. San Francisco: Prima Publishing.

Levinson, Jay Conrad. 1987. *Guerrilla Marketing*. New York: Houghton-Mifflin.

McKay, Matt, and Pat Fanning. 1992. *Self-Esteem*. Oakland: New Harbinger Publications.

Peters, Tom, and Robert Waterman. 1982. *In Search of Excellence*. New York: Warner Books.

Robbins, Tony. 1996. *Personal Power II*. Robbins Research International (audiotape series).

Robbins, Tony. 1991. *Awaken the Giant Within*. New York: Simon & Schuster.

Zigler, Zig. 1998. *Success for Dummies*. Foster City, CA: IDG Books.

Embracing Your Strengths, Accepting Your Limitations

And if not now, when?

—The Talmud

If you grew up in a problem-focused family, you were trained at an early age to become a faultfinder. You will unconsciously look at the world through a filter of problem-focused perception. Your self-assessment will be based on what is wrong rather than what is right.

This next exercise will ask you to make a list of ten strengths you have. It may be difficult at first and you may even have to ask a close friend for some feedback on this:

Exercise: Ten Strengths

Here are some of Jerry's answers:

1. I am a good listener.

2. I am a good athlete

3. I am intelligent.

4. I am funny at times.

5. I am sensitive.

6. I am creative.

7. I am responsible.

8. I am a good speaker.

9. I can be a lot of fun.

10. I am a good father.

Now it's your turn.

1. _____

2. _____

3. _____

4. _____

5. _____

6. _____

7. _____

8. _____

9. _____

10. _____

Building Your Confidence

Exercise: Ten Accomplishments You Are Proud Of

This exercise may be uncomfortable for you to do or complete if you learned that self-acknowledgment is bragging. You may pride yourself on being humble or even self-effacing. However, this will only diminish your sense of self-pride or competence. Learn to tell the truth about yourself and that includes your strengths and accomplishments. Celebrate your accomplishments while you learn that what you focus on expands!

1. _____

2. _____

3. _____

4. _____

5. _____

6. _____

7. _____

8. _____

9. _____

10. _____

Note: These do not have to be front-page items in the *New York Times*.

Here are some examples:

- I won second prize on my seventh grade poetry contest.

- I help inner city children on Saturdays.

- I got promoted to Account Executive.

- I ran in the Chicago marathon.

- I have two beautiful children.

- I learned to play "Silent Night" on the piano.

- I earned $60,000 last year.

- I was starting first baseman on my sixth-grade team.

Shattering Limiting Beliefs

I don't like work—no man does—but I like what is in work—the chance to find yourself. Your own reality for yourself, not for others; what no other man can ever know.

—Joseph Conrad

Rich, a forty-six-year-old consultant, recalls his breakthrough around physical fitness. "I have been kind of stuck for years now regarding fitness. I do get to the health club about three times a week, but in my hour there, I rarely work up much of a sweat. I usually spend about twenty minutes walking on the treadmill, then I do some weights. One day I was discussing this with my friend Brian, who always seems to be in better shape than me. He said he goes on the treadmill for about twenty-five minutes and after the first ten minutes, he speeds it up to 6.5 mph and stays there for about another fifteen minutes. I said, "I don't do that because my calves get tight when I start to run, and I guess I'm just not much of a runner." Brian responded, "When I start running after a break, my calves get tight, too, so I stretch them out and when they get tight again I just keep going and burn through the pain and it gets better."

I thought to myself, "Just burn through it and it gets better?" Well, the very next time I got on the treadmill, after about ten minutes, I kicked it up to 6.5 mph and it was pure exhilaration. Yes, my calves got a little tight, but I heard Brian's voice saying "Just burn through it!" And I did. It was by far the best workout I've ever had and I've been able to keep up and even expand on that pace ever since."

Rich's problem was not in his physical abilities, it was in his limiting belief about his capacity as a runner. As soon as he could develop a new vision based on his friend Brain's experience, he was able to examine his beliefs. Then his proactive action step of actually discovering that he could run at 6.5 mph allowed him to succeed at expanding his workout.

The two most important steps in creating real change in your life are first to decide to clarify your intentions and then to act on more constructive and empowering thoughts and actions.

1. Realize these new messages and actions are about *who you want to be,* not who you are today.

2. Phrase your messages to yourself in the present tense. Instead of saying, "I plan to work out three times this week," say, "I work out three times a week."

3. When you create your own messages, get behind them emotionally. Feel their real value for your growth and future fulfillment.

4. Make your new thoughts and actions attainable and realistic.

5. Create some small changes that you can succeed at today. "I will smile at my spouse and encourage him/her to tell me how the day went."

6. Review your hoped-for changes before you go to bed each night so that your subconscious can work on them throughout the night.

7. Put the new thoughts and actions you are working on 3 x 5 index cards so that you can look at them throughout the day until you have programmed them into your daily life.

New Thoughts and New Actions

I am still learning.

—Michelangelo

Positive Affirmations You Can Say to Yourself

- I have a unique voice and the right to express it. I don't need to hear what others think. I need to hear myself think.

- I give myself permission to succeed in all I do. I deserve to be a tremendous success in all areas of my life and to experience the rich rewards of this success.

- I can create financial success by changing my thoughts and taking consistent action.

- Responsibility is a value I can learn by practicing it every day.

- I have the ability to surpass all my past levels of accomplishment.

- I realize that failure is an event, not a person. I can begin new patterns of success today.

- Responsibility is the ability to respond creatively to each new moment.

- There are no mistakes, only lessons. I know great results come from a series of small steps.

- There are 525,600 minutes in each year. I can choose to be conscious as to how I spend these minutes.

- I have the right and the ability to create the life of my dreams.

Positive Things You Can Do for Yourself

- Commit to doing a simple and enjoyable project around the house and complete it in a timely manner. For example, paint the hallway near the roof deck.

- Make a list of five tasks you are avoiding and finish one this week. For example, "Clean and organize the desk in my office."

- Make a list of five strengths you have in the area of work and share this list with a trusted friend. For example, "I am punctual, sensitive, reliable, intelligent, and creative."

- Become aware of how you reel in helpers to rescue you. Take back one of these tasks and do it yourself. For example, "I let my wife clean the house. I can get more involved in the daily cleaning."

- Remember to acknowledge your small successes. For example, "I finished my taxes on time."

- Listen to inspirational speakers regularly. Find and read motivational books.

Do the difficult tasks *first* so that you can feel a sense of pride in completion and so you can fully enjoy the time when you are relaxing.

6

When You Can't Find the Right Person

*The Fifth Key: Intimacy—
Learn How to Achieve Closeness
and Be Emotionally Honest*

Understanding the Key Issue

"He's smart, but he doesn't make a good salary."

"She's pretty, but she has no interest in sports and I hate her friends."

"He's everything I want, but I'm not attracted to him physically."

"He's got a great sense of humor, I have a great time with him, but he's twenty-eight and still living at home with his mother."

Sound familiar? Obviously we have a right to our preferences. If you've had several relationships that were lacking something you needed, it is quite normal to move on in

the hope that you'll find what's missing with someone else. But what if we find that, honestly—no one is ever enough? What if there's always something missing?

Ken is a case in point. His relationship with Sherry didn't end with bitter words. It just faded away in an uneasy silence. Ken recalls, "There were phone calls when we had little to say, dates where we watched videos, made love out of habit, and fell asleep with our backs to each other. I know I spent the last month we were together fantasizing about being somewhere else whenever I was with her, and I'm sure she was doing that, too."

Their parting was amicable, the emotional bruises few. Still, something is bothering Ken deeply. "I'm thirty-five. Okay, maybe Sherry and I didn't hook up, but I'm beginning to wonder, is it ever going to happen for me?" What Ken really wants to know is this: "Is it me? Am I doing something wrong? Why can't I find the right person?"

The Relationship Questionnaire

When Ken came to us with those questions, we gave him the next quiz to help him clarify his feelings. You can take this quiz either while you're still in a relationship or after a relationship has ended by changing the phrases to the past tense. Some of our clients have taken the quiz based on a number of different relationships, one for each person with whom they were involved. The comparisons were always interesting and, sometimes, those who took the quiz gained insight into their relationships.

Read each statement and put an X in the appropriate box (1 = strongly disagree, 2 = disagree somewhat, 3 = neutral, 4 = moderately agree, 5 = strongly agree).

How Strong Is Your Relationship?	1	2	3	4	5
1. Each day I look forward to talking with my partner.					
2. We have a lot of interests in common.					
3. I am physically attracted to my partner.					
4. I feel it is safe to be vulnerable in my relationship.					
5. We have fun playing together.					
6. When I am away from my partner for a day, I miss him/her.					
7. I am happy to be in this relationship.					
8. We resolve conflicts rather than build resentments.					
9. I feel supported and understood.					

10. I feel my partner brings a lot to the relationship.					
11. I feel proud to introduce my partner to my family.					
12. I feel proud to introduce my partner to my friends.					
13. I am comfortable with my partner's past.					
14. I feel my partner listens to me.					
15. My partner respects my need for space.					
16. I feel we each give equally to each other, if not every day, then in the long run.					
17. I can say "I love you" easily to my partner.					
18. Sexually, my partner and I are compatible.					
19. I feel accepted for who I really am.					
20. I don't wonder, "Is there someone better out there for me?" because I'm content working on this relationship and taking it as far as it can go.					

Your total score: _____

Evaluating Your Score

80–100: Your relationship is strong. You and your partner connect deeply and have a lot in common. This chapter will support your continued path of insight and self-discovery.

60–80: Your relationships have themes of connection and of hesitancy. The exercises in this chapter will help you to discover whether you are distancing others because of unresolved issues or if you would truly be more compatible with someone else.

40–60: Your score reflects a moderate degree of relationship dissatisfaction. It will be important for you to do the following exercises to determine exactly where the problem lies. This chapter will give your concrete tools for building intimacy and connection.

0–40: Your score reflects a significant struggle with relationships. You deserve more satisfaction. The key questions to ask yourself are these: "Is there some way I am attracting this type of discontent to my life? What do I need to develop in myself to achieve more satisfying and joyful relationships?"

*The easiest kind of relationship for me is with ten
thousand people, the hardest is with one.*

—Joan Baez

Recycling the Past: How Your History Affects Your Current Relationship Choices

Gail, thirty-four, moves with an easy grace and calm manner as she makes the rounds through the hospital where she is a resident. Her attitude of self-confidence is reassuring to her patients. Gail is the type of person others feel safe relying on.

The man Gail dates readily admits that he relies on her, too. He depends on her advice. He relies on her organized apartment, her efficiency in the kitchen, her knack for making him comfortable. Yet for the last two weeks he's been distant, self-absorbed, and angry. She can feel him pulling away.

Gail is upset, but more with herself than him. "I always go for the type of guy who seems to need me. Jim was between jobs when we met, unsettled and pretty down on himself. I was there for him and I really believed he loved me. The arguments we're having lately are because he never listens to *me*. When I found out that he didn't even know where I went to medical school, I couldn't believe it. We had a blow out and his whole point was, 'What difference does it make if I don't know?' He actually told me he thinks I'm *needy*. I was stunned. The only reason he knows the name of the hospital I work at is that he calls me there. I know this guy's shoe size, for Chrissakes."

When Gail looks back at her last four relationships, this recent quarrel is really not so surprising. She's attracted to selfish, arrogant men who believe that anyone who makes them focus on anything but their own desire for attention is a needy person. Looking back at her childhood, the whole issue of Gail's needs and how few people have been available to meet them looms large.

"My mother has multiple sclerosis. That's what made me want to become a doctor in the first place. A lot of the responsibility for my mother and my brothers fell on me. My brothers were always in trouble. They probably needed a stronger mother but she didn't have the energy to discipline them. My father was busy putting food on the table and paying the bills. Both of my parents told me every day that they were proud that I wasn't like my brothers."

Being self-reliant and thus supposedly "needless" earned Gail her parents' love and respect. She got attention for her outstanding report cards, prize-winning science fair projects, crowd-pleasing piano recitals. This "style" of relating to those she cared about followed her into adulthood. Today, as an adult, she wows her partners with her intelligence, her flawless apartment, her skills in the kitchen, her excellent advice on their troubles at work. Then the moment of truth comes. "I stop cooking dinner and say let's go out for dinner. Or, I stop wanting to listen to another long drawn-out discussion of his year-end review, and I want to talk about my work. That's when things begin to go sour."

The trouble is, no matter how "need-less" any of us tries to appear, we all have emotional needs. There will come a time during all of our "giving" that we finally say, "Hey, me too." Often this occurs when we begin to feel confident in another person's love, as Gail began to feel with Jim. But when she said, "Me too," he backed off. He was looking for a provider. He argued that Gail had "changed." She wasn't the "strong woman" he had known.

It became obvious to Gail that she has never felt loved just for being who she is. What she gets from other people often feels like applause for a very good show. It leaves her feeling empty, and looking for completion through "the right person."

If you are struggling to find "the right person," ask yourself the following questions:

- Is there something familiar about my current relationship struggles?

- Do I seem to attract the same types of unhappy relationships?

- Do I feel free to really be myself in a relationship?

- Is there always something missing in my relationships?

If you are able to notice a theme or pattern that keeps recurring, the odds are good that you are recycling limiting patterns from your past. Don't be discouraged, most people do this. However, you can change these patterns. There's an old saying, "When the student is ready, the teacher appears."

> *The space for what you want is already*
> *filled with what you settle for instead.*
>
> —Stephan C. Paul

All the Good Ones Are Boring: Are You Attracted to Impossible Relationships?

"Ken, tell me the truth. Do you think I'm being paranoid?" Kristin asked, grabbing the Kleenex he handed her, and wiping away the tears that came so easily these days. "This woman called Alan four times yesterday. Now he tells me she's going to Las Vegas with him for a week. When I asked him why they were staying through the weekend if it was just business, do you know what he did? He slapped twenty dollars down on the table, and walked out of the restaurant, leaving me sitting there. Can you believe that?"

"I believe it," Ken said quietly. He got up and walked toward the kitchen, and Kristin could hear him opening a bottle of wine. As he returned, two glasses in hand, she thought for the hundredth time, "Whey can't I fall in love with someone like him? Why am I always attracted to jerks like Alan?" But for Kristen, there's no "chemistry" with men like Ken. A nice, ordinary man who is good for her and good to her arouses none of the lust that men like Alan excite in her.

In our practice we've heard dozen of reasons for staying in tortuous relationships, each time to devastating effects: "I know underneath all the bad treatment I get, he really

does love me" and "Even though she's not trustworthy, she can be so sweet at times" are typical. The real reasons for being drawn to impossible relationships often go deeper. Sometimes involvement in a traumatic relationship is an unconscious way of trying to re-create a struggle from the past and to finally triumph over it in the present.

Karen, a woman involved in a devastating relationship with a married man, had been a child who was virtually ignored by her parents who doted on her older brother. Her brother was popular, attractive, a star on the football field, and Karen trailed after him in school, often befriended by girls who befriended her only to get close to her brother.

Children of unavailable or absent parents often become adults who need constant reassurance. They may spend their lives compulsively trying to overcome the early identities given to them by their families by striving desperately to prove that they are good enough. But, at the same time, they are incapable of trusting another person's willingness to love them.

For many people, relationships with unavailable people are comfortable because the feelings that are generated are so familiar. The struggle to conquer the unavailable lover is really about the unconscious need to overcome the indifference of some significant person in the past and to bolster a shaky identity.

Other people are drawn to impossible relationships for the distractions they create. When you're constantly wondering whether you should pick up the phone—or let it ring to make him jealous—when you're always dreaming up things to say or do to make things right, all the drama leaves you with little energy to contemplate questions such as, "Am I happy with myself? Am I satisfied with where I'm going in my life?" An obsession with another person's behavior can distract you from your own problems, which may be massive: long-standing depression, feelings of guilt or self-hatred, or behavior compulsions that are triggered by diminished self-esteem.

Most often, however, the penchant for impossible relationships is a cover for a deep ambivalence about being intimate with anyone at all. You may unconsciously choose the unavailable partner because of the limited amount of closeness he or she is capable of providing, not in spite of it. Distance is what is comfortable. Your ability to be close, to be honest, to accept another person's love, may have been severely damaged by something in the past which defeated you. You don't know if you could handle another person's commitment if you got it. This is why many people admit that when their pursuit of the unavailable person is finally successful, they begin to lose interest.

If you're involved in an impossible relationship, the most important questions to ask yourself are, "What do I need from this person? What am I not getting that's making me so miserable?"

"I just want him to appreciate me," Lisa, thirty-two, admitted. "I just want a little respect. I need to know that I matter to him." But what Lisa wants from him she has the power to give herself. She can start appreciating herself and treating herself as if she matters. She can learn to become her own provider of love and respect. She can stop chasing after an elusive person and learn to hold still and develop a deeper relationship with herself. Only then will her relationships with others be based on the excitement of shared intimacy rather than on the drama of the conquest of an unavailable lover.

When Intimacy Doesn't Come Easily: Why It's Never Enough

We sleep in separate rooms, we have dinner apart, we take separate vacations—we're doing everything we can to keep our marriage together.

—Rodney Dangerfield

In *Perfect Women* (1988), Collette Dowling wrote about women who can never find the right man and called it "shopping for a star." "What can he do for me? is the hidden pre-eminent question for a women who feels inadequate," Dowling writes. "If she thinks he has enough to compensate for what she's missing, 'love' may follow."

Dowling could also have been writing about men, because both sexes can fall into the habit of searching for perfection in another person. What you may be unconsciously looking for isn't for someone to love you, but someone to make you feel stronger in the places you feel weakest. It's often the shortcomings you perceive in yourself that make you so critical of others. It may seem that you can never find anyone smart, rich, exciting, or beautiful enough to compensate for what you feel is lacking in yourself. What you are looking for is someone to complete you.

It can be difficult to see, but the "not enough" we judge in the other person often comes from within. What might be the cause? In the sections that follow, we'll look at the most frequent cause, which is the unconscious fear of intimacy

The Unconscious Fear of Intimacy

The notion that many people have unconscious fears of intimacy has been pointed out so often it has become a cliché. As one client put it, "A friend of mine said to me, 'Maybe you get into these impossible relationships because you really don't want to commit to anyone.' I think that's bullshit. I've been trying to get married for the last ten years. I've done the fix-ups, the personal ads, the classes where-you-might-meet-someone-who-shares-your-interests. And I've invested time and money in workshops for singles, learning to be more accepting of myself. I supported my last girlfriend for six months before we broke up because I kept believing the relationship could still work out. Do I sound to you like someone who is afraid of intimacy?"

Let's change the vocabulary for a moment. Do you find yourself very protective of yourself in the beginning of your relationships? Do you listen carefully to what the other person may say in an offhand manner, and then find yourself analyzing what was said later? Do you make silent cost-benefit analyses of what it would be like to be with this person before you've really gotten to know him or her?

Do you become angry easily and very wary of being taken advantage of, especially after you've had sex with a new partner? If the person said he/she was going to call and then calls a day late, does that secretly make you seethe and start you on a spiral of internal recriminations to the tune of, "If that person really cared, he/she would have called when they said they would?"

Such feelings often arise due to a fear of intimacy. It is important to note here that fear of intimacy is not unjustified. Falling in love does leave you exposed and vulnerable. You might care more than the other person does in the beginning, thus leaving yourself open to disappointment. There are healthy fears of intimacy, such as those that make you give a wide berth to people who aren't emotionally available for relationships, for example. This differs from chronic fear of intimacy which actually can bring out the worst in your partners and leave you feeling unappreciated, inept, and unloved.

Shannon met Bill in a volleyball league that met every Saturday morning at a local beach during the summer. He was patient with her wobbly serve. He cheered her good plays and grinned supportively when the ball ended up at her feet. They both loved jazz, browsing the Net, big dogs, baked potatoes with yogurt, and sleeping until noon on Sundays. It was a summer romance that didn't fade in the fall, but grew deeper. By the New Year they both said, "I love you." But in March, Shannon became restless. She started noticing things—like his socks, for instance. They never matched and they had holes in them. In fact, he definitely didn't have the clothes thing together. Worse, he didn't have the career thing together, either. "He was selling a line of gift items for his uncle. He could have done great but he really just looked at it as maintenance money so he'd be free to do what he loved to do, which was to play with his computer."

Shannon was no career whiz herself. She was always between jobs and hard put to make the rent. "But it started to bother me that Bill didn't have more motivation. He used to say, 'Stick with me—we'll never starve.' But I wanted more than that."

To give Bill credit, he tried to please Sharon. He increased his sales territory. He spent more time at work. But it wasn't enough for her. It ended one night in an ugly argument when Bill said, "You don't want me. You want my father. Someone who's going to work himself into a heart attack at age forty-five and never have time to enjoy life. That ain't me, babe."

A year later Shannon admits, "I miss him terribly. The funny thing is, he was making decent money. It really wasn't the money. It was a feeling of being connected to someone for the rest of my life, for better or for worse. I think I doubted myself. If he wasn't going to have it all together what was going to happen to me with all of my issues?"

In the end it came down to trust. Fear of intimacy usually comes down to that basic issue. Love and trust should go hand in hand, but for many people they are two very different things:

- You can love someone, but believe they'll leave you once they know it—fear of abandonment.

- You can adore someone but believe that they won't adore you once they really know you—fear of exposure.

- You can feel a strong attraction and want to be with someone until you begin to feel smothered by their needs and constant attention—fear of engulfment.

What's difficult to comprehend is that the other person usually doesn't cause these fears. Yes, he wears ugly socks. Yes, she smooches her cat in a way that makes you cringe. He doesn't charm your friends, but that isn't what gives rise to these fears. They were there already, probably as far back as your childhood.

The following questionnaire will allow you to determine which fears are holding you back from experiencing greater closeness and intimacy.

The Intimacy Inventory

Questionnaire

Assign a number that best describes how you feel concerning each of the following statements. Base your answers on what has been true for you for *the greater part of your life*. What comes most quickly to your mind is usually the best answer.

0 = definitely not me, 1 = mildly disagree, 2 = neutral, 3 = mildly agree, 4 = definitely me

1. Are you concerned that if you truly reveal yourself to another person, they will leave you?	
2. Do you fear that if someone really knew you that they wouldn't like you?	
3. Do you have an uneasy feeling that people will smother you if you get too close?	
4. Did a parent physically or emotionally abandon you in your childhood?	
5. When you were younger were you teased or shamed for your feelings or needs?	
6. As a child, did you feel that one of your parents or significant caretakers was overly involved in your life?	
7. If you have a conflict with your partner and he or she pulls away do you feel a sense of panic?	
8. If your lover did a background check on you that was really on the mark, would you want to hide?	
9. Do you find yourself needing more space in relationships, once another person tells you that they really care about you?	
10. When the person you've been involved with for half a year says that he/she's taking a vacation with friends that don't include you, do you get angry?	
11. Would you show your checkbook to your lover?	
12. Do you feel smothered when in the first few weeks of a relationship your partner wants you to call every day?	

Scoring

1. Fear of Abandonment (Add your scores for questions 1, 4, 7, and 10.)
   Total _____

2. Fear of Exposure (Add your scores for questions 2, 5, 8 and 11.)
   Total _____

3. Fear of Engulfment (Add your scores for questions 3, 6, 9, and 12.)
Total _____

If you score higher than 10 on any of the three fears, this is a strong indication that this fear is creating a block that prevents you from becoming more fully intimate with others. In the next section we'll examine specific fears more thoroughly.

Understanding the Three Primary Fears of Intimacy

*Our opinion of people depends less upon what we
see in them than upon what they make us see in ourselves.*

—Sarah Grand

The Fear of Abandonment

If I let you really know me, you would leave me.

For many people the fear of abandonment is a primary fear. It comes from emotional or physical abandonment in early life. One obvious example is the child who grows up in a home where a parent has deserted the family by leaving the home (physical abandonment). This often happens without the children even being informed that the parent is leaving or has left. A less obvious example occurs when a primary caretaker withdraws emotionally from the child, that is, the caretaker becomes cold or gets angry when the child expresses his or her needs (emotional abandonment).

These types of experiences set up an expectation or fear that other significant people will do the same. To defend against this painful possibility, children build psychological defenses. Some of these defenses may be: 1) building emotional "walls" that prevent others from becoming intimate; 2) playing the role of caretaker or people-pleaser to ensure that others will never leave; 3) leaving others first.

For those who fear abandonment, the fear can be triggered by even the slightest suggestion of a significant person pulling away, a darkened mood, a critical remark, or a partner's need for personal space.

The Fear of Engulfment

If I allow you to be close to me, you would smother me.

Will I have to give up all my freedom? Will I lose myself if I fall in love? The fear of engulfment represents a projected fear of being smothered psychologically by another. It is a common fear of children who grew up with controlling or needy parents. Children with these types of parents become extensions for their parent's needs. Instead of receiving validation, feedback, and acceptance, they are given subtle messages such as *Make mommy and daddy happy. Do what we say or else disaster will follow you.*

Unempathic or intrusive styles of parenting cause children to adapt their true needs to meet the parent's agenda. Every child instinctively knows that physical and psychological safety is the first order of importance. But while the child complies with the parents' rules of safety, at the same time the child is building defenses to protect himself or herself from this form of engulfment. The primary defense is to push others away—directly or indirectly. This survival strategy becomes habitual and is repeated endlessly in other relationships.

The Fear of Exposure

If I let you really know me, you would find me deficient.

The fear of exposure is the third primary fear of intimacy. This fear is born from growing up in a shaming or judgmental environment. Scornful criticism might have been directed at you frequently: "You are really stupid, what's wrong with you?" Or malicious criticism might have been aimed at others outside the family "Look at your cousin, she's so fat." Or, "Your uncle has been a loser since he was in high school." When we hear such messages over and over again, we tend to internalize them as truths. Then people often become their own harshest critics, hoping to beat others to the punch.

One way we protect ourselves from anticipated criticism is to reveal very little of ourselves. The less others know, the less they are likely to hurt us. Unfortunately, when you hide parts of yourself, you are unable to have the experience of full acceptance. Your inner feelings of shame never get revealed or healed. And you never really allow yourself to get close or feel any sense of true intimacy. We call this the subtle art of distancing.

The Subtle Art of Distancing

Happiness is having a large, loving, caring, close-knit family in another city.

—George Burns

Barry, thirty-four, came into therapy reporting a string of relationship failures and a generalized feeling of depression. Despite his moodiness he was a very likable guy with many strengths. Yet as he told his family history it became clear that his mother's death when he was seven years old was still an unresolved and lingering source of grief.

He approached adult relationships with caution, fearing a repetition of his original loss if he allowed himself to become truly close. He also felt that if a woman got to really know him, she would find him inadequate in some way (as he had felt when his mother died).

As a result of his mother's death, Barry developed an arsenal of distancing techniques at a very early age that would send others the message *Don't get too close*. His typical distancing strategies (often unconscious) were as follows: not sharing his true feelings, sarcasm, not calling others back in a timely manner, showing up late, and isolating himself at home.

Generally, distancing techniques are habits of behavior used to protect ourselves, although we may do so unconsciously. The problem with this type of protective strategy is that it does not allow safe people to be trusted. It is a kind of all-or-nothing thinking that locks the doors on all visitors.

In therapy, Barry learned to connect his current relationship struggles to the unresolved grief in his past. He learned to share his true feelings and to examine the distortions in his thinking as they were projected onto his current relationships. In group therapy, he learned to risk being more honest and to reveal more of his underlying depression and to reach for support when necessary. At the end of two years of therapy he was able to enter relationships more fully and to let go of his distancing techniques.

How Do You Distance People?

The following list illustrates common distancing techniques used by many people. Examine this list and notice those that have been pointed out to you as typical of your behavior, or that you feel you most identify with. Place a checkmark next to the statements that apply to you. Do you:

Need to be right?	
Work all the time?	
Intellectualize your relationships?	
Wait for people to read your mind?	
Complain a lot?	
Focus on problems in most of your conversations?	
Make jokes at inappropriate times?	
Act in a passive-aggressive manner?	
Get irritable with others often?	
Get depressed often?	
Talk too much?	
Use sarcasm a lot?	
Withhold affection or sex?	
Avoid telling the truth?	

Wait for other people to recognize that you are angry or hurt, and for them to apologize?	
Stay high on alcohol or drugs?	
Build boundaries around yourself through excess weight?	
Arrive late consistently?	
React intensely to criticism?	

Scoring

If you've checked more than five items in the questionnaire, ask yourself if you often feel lonely or disconnected from other people. The belief that abandonment, engulfment, or exposure is the natural result of intimacy may cause you to dismiss or repulse other people without even being aware of what you are doing.

Why It Will Never Be Enough

You cannot find a person who will erase your fears of abandonment, exposure, or engulfment. You have to do that work for yourself. No one can do it for you. More than eliminating these very human fears, you're going to have to learn how to work through them and sometimes around them.

You may believe that you are searching for the right person, but consider the possibility that you may be searching for something else: a feeling of value, proof that you aren't invisible, and proof that you are important.

You may also be searching for a sense of security and competence. When you focus on relationships as a mean to this end, you set yourself up for disappointment because you end up focusing on finding an emotional provider, rather than on learning how to provide for yourself. Only when you can provide emotional sustenance to yourself will you be able to share yourself with a partner.

Rx: Building Intimacy

Life without love is like a tree without blossom and fruit.

—Kahlil Gibran

Your Key Questions

1. What's holding me back from opening my heart more fully?
   (E.g., *I was rejected by my first love; my family teased me whenever I shared my feelings; I fear that people will criticize me or leave me if I really let them know me.*)

   _____

   _____

   _____

   _____

   _____

2. What did I learn from my family of origin about marriage and relationships? How might this be affecting me today?
   (E.g., *marriage means losing your freedom; don't show your feelings; women (or men) will smother you.*)

   _____

   _____

   _____

   _____

   _____

3. What are the qualities I really value in a relationship?
   (E.g., *honesty, sincerity, optimism, playfulness.*)

   _____

   _____

   _____

_____

_____

_____

4. What qualities do I need to develop in myself to attract the relationship I desire? (E.g., *I need to practice being more loving, to express my needs with others, admit my mistakes rather than being defensive.*)

_____

_____

_____

_____

_____

5. Am I willing to take risks and create more intimate connections with others? If not, why not? If so, what can I do this week? (E.g., *I have always protected myself by being a loner. However, I am now willing to risk initiating plans with friends because I now believe I'd rather be rejected once in a while than to be lonely all the time.*)

_____

_____

_____

_____

_____

See How Your Symptoms Serve You

You may have mixed feelings about giving up your cautiousness in relationships. You've been hurt before and you've found ways of protecting yourself by keeping others at bay. In this section you will uncover your unique protection strategy. Remember the first step to creating intimacy is to become clear about how you defeat the possibility of intimacy occurring in your life.

Some symptoms of using protective strategies to defeat the possibility of intimacy are as follows:

- Short relationships that end in bitterness

- Never feeling anyone else is enough

- Nit-picking and breaking up and regretting it later

These may be your attempts at solving some very basic issues. Consider the following table and ask yourself if your behavior corresponds to some of these symptoms and their protective functions.

Symptom	Protective Function
1. I can't find the right person.	I don't have to "be" the right person. I don't have to give and I don't get hurt.
2. Desire for unavailable people.	"Safe passion" manages fears of intimacy. I feel—passion—but it's because I'm always wishing, hoping, and aching for this indifferent person to validate my feelings.
3. I need someone rich, beautiful, famous, who has a perfect body, etc.	To complete myself. An attempt to raise self-esteem by attaching to someone stronger. "If you can attract such a special person, you must be special."

Create New Choices

"I'm always recruiting and rejecting the applicants," one client admitted with a smile. No one knew more than he did about where to meet women and how to coax them into his life. It was the next step—moving beyond attraction into the deeper passion of knowing another person intimately and being known by that person that really eluded him.

With therapy, he became able to look at his specific behaviors and to create new choices. So can you. Let's look at his chart.

Symptom	Protective Function	Downside to This Solution	New Choices
After I have sex with a women I lose interest in her.	I can share something I'm good at—sex—and avoid what I've been told I'm bad at—listening, caring, and working through problems. I never have to let anyone see the parts of myself I have doubts about.	Feelings of emptiness. Banal sex; a couple of scary scrapes with women who became vindictive after being dropped.	Stay out of bed. Work on my fears of intimacy in therapy or by sharing with a trusted friend. Allowing things to happen gradually.

I set up conflicts in order to sabotage relationships. Then, the minute the woman is out the door, I seem to love her more intensely than I did when I was with her.	Leave someone before she leaves you. Safe passion. No risks. Then, I feel committed to someone who's gone.	No fulfillment. Regret. Sadness.	Don't get involved so quickly that I hit all my triggers in the first two weeks. Work through my bitterness about my parents marriage— maybe talk to my sister about the divorce to find out what really happened.

Exercise: Finding New Solutions

Now it's your turn.

- In the first column, write the symptoms you identified in "See How Your Symptoms Serve You."

- In the second column, write the original protective function of this strategy.

- In the third column, write the downside to this solution.

- In the fourth column, write a more effective solution to this problem

Symptom	Protective Function	Downside to This Solution	New Choices
1.			
2.			
3.			
4.			
5.			

Visualize Your Relationship

What you can believe you can achieve.

Now that you are beginning to see how your past survival strategies have shaped your current relationship patterns, it is time to break free and create a new more positive picture for yourself. Close your eyes and take a deep breath. Imagine there are no fears to hold you back, no chains to the past. Create a vision of your ideal relationship. See this picture in your mind as clearly as possible. What qualities does this person have? What does he/she look like? How does he/she treat you? How are you different in this relationship? What qualities would you like to develop in yourself that this relationship will encourage?

Allow yourself to gently let go of any resistance to this visualization exercise that you may have. If your images are not yet clear, come back to this exercise regularly. Work on creating a clear, fully realized picture. Your positive intentions will guide you to increased clarity.

Now write the thoughts and pictures that came to you during this meditation in the space provided below.

_____

_____

_____

_____

_____

Using Relationships to Develop Aspects of Yourself

Everything that irritates us about others
can lead us to an understanding of ourselves.

—Carl Jung

He wasn't making enough money? Perhaps you need to develop a sense of greater abundance yourself, or to work on ways to create more income and security for yourself. She wasn't attractive enough? How attractive do you feel? Are you happy with what you see in the mirror? Are you confident in yourself when you're around other people?

Often, what's missing in relationships are reflections of what we most fear is missing in ourselves. He may not seem as if he'd be a great father. But would you be a great

mother? She's too entangled with her family business. Have you learned to set boundaries within your own family?

Make a list of the last three people you were romantically involved with. Next to the names on this list write what went wrong and what was missing. As you ponder this, consider the notion that everything you wrote next to the names may be, in some way, a reflection of something you want or need to develop in yourself.

Example

Sara, thirty-four, account executive says, "John was controlling, arrogant, and self-centered. I seemed to always end up doing things his way. I tried to please him any way I could. I figured one day my turn would come. It never did. This is such a familiar pattern. I end up giving the guy everything I've got, hoping and wishing that someday he'll see how much I'm giving to him, and then he'll start giving something back to me. It never happens."

Reflection: "I never really assert my own needs. It feels selfish to ask other people to do things my way. I hope men will read my mind. Sometimes I give and give but it's really not about making him happy, it's about making him see how great I am so he'll give something back to me. That's the way I try to achieve some sense of control. I need to develop my sense of self-importance and skills of assertion."

Example

Mark, twenty-six, real estate salesperson says, "Jane was just like all the other women whom I have dated, wanting more from me than I want to give. These relationships always feel smothering to me. When I say I want some space, they all act hurt. Like I'm supposed to feel guilty—and I do. It's just like when I was a kid. If I didn't do everything my mother's way she'd be hurt. I just can't stand to see a woman cry. Women seem so needy to me I just want to get away."

Reflection: "I have a hard time saying no without feeling guilty. On a deep level I feel responsible for other people's happiness as I did with my mother. I hide my true feelings and run away from women who seem needy. But the truth is, I want a woman who will give to me and not ask for a lot back. In that way, I'm the needy one. I need to take less responsibility for others' happiness. I need to assert my needs fully and to learn to negotiate healthy boundaries that will allow time together and guilt-free time for personal space."

These clients did not come to these insights overnight. It takes a lot of renewed confidence to admit that you might be the needy one or the arrogant one and then to commit to move on from that point toward a more fulfilling way of relating.

Exercise: What Do Your Relationships Reflect?

The typical qualities of partner I tend to attract are these:
(E.g., *self-absorbed, arrogant, wants a lot of space, controlling, critical.*)

_____

_____

_____

_____

These are the qualities that I need to develop in myself:
(E.g., *ability to identify and assert my own needs; stop playing the caretaker; understand and manage my fears of intimacy; develop other areas of my life—work and play.*)

_____

_____

_____

_____

_____

Understanding the Origins of Your Relationship Patterns

Exercise: Your Childhood Wounds

The following exercise will help you to understand the exact nature of your relationship patterns. In the first column, write down the most painful relationship memories of your childhood. In the second column, write down the conclusion you reached about people as a result of these events. In the third column, write down how you protect yourself from never having to experience this pain again (this is your solution to the problem).

Example

Childhood Wounds	My Conclusion About This	My "Solution" (Self-Defeating Pattern)
Mom died when I was seven.	People will leave me. I can't trust relationships	I never get really close to anyone.
Dad was always critical of me, nothing I did was ever good enough for him.	Nothing I do will ever be enough.	I procrastinate or give up before I start.

My father left mom when I was two.	I have to be the responsible parent.	I always stay in charge, never trusting others.
My parents felt that anyone I met was never good enough for me.	I shouldn't trust my instincts.	I am very critical of people I date. It starts out hot and heavy and then I lose interest.
My family was always fighting and criticizing others.	It's not safe to express myself.	I am a people-pleaser, I never tell others what I really feel.

Your Self-Defeating Pattern Assignment

Fill in the three-column table below with the specifics from your own life.

Childhood Wounds	My Conclusion About This	My "Solution" (Self-Defeating Pattern)

Revisiting Your Parents' Marriage

What kinds of pictures do you have stored in your mind? Like it or not, our first and most impressionable picture of intimacy and love is our parents' marriage. As children we learn about love by watching our parents relate to each other. Some messages are verbal: *I*

love you . . . I'm so glad you're home . . . You're such a nag . . . You're impossible . . . Some messages are nonverbal: the display of affection through touch, smiles, and warmth, or a cold avoidance of each other, and the sharp words and tones of criticism and anger.

Tom, a twenty-nine-year-old salesman, recalls, "I always had the feeling that my father gave up his real desires in life to get married and have a family. I remember him as tired and depressed most of the time. We never talked very much. But I do remember the time he told me that he had studied art in college and that he had won several awards for his paintings. When he got married, he had to give art up for good to 'get a real job' to support his family. My sense is that he gave up his passion in life for us. I can't remember a time when he really spoke up for what he wanted. He always seemed to give in to my mother. I'm scared that if I ever get married, the same thing will happen to me. I associate marriage with losing myself. I don't want to end up like my dad."

Janet, thirty-seven, remembers her parents' marriage as being perfect. When she was close to getting married herself recently, she was very surprised at her mother's confession: "Marriage means sacrifice. I have to be ready to go with your father's plans when he walks in the door. When you were children I had to make sure your toys were picked up and you were clean and happy when he came home. He couldn't tolerate the mess. He didn't want to be distracted from his work. I was always tired, and I never had any time for myself." Janet was amazed to learn how much energy her mother had needed to create the picture of a perfect marriage.

Answering the following questions will help you to understand how your parents' marriage may have shaped your relationship expectations.

Were your parents in love with each other?

_____

_____

How did they show their love?

_____

_____

What was your father's role in the marriage?

_____

_____

What was your mother's role in the marriage?

_____

_____

What did you learn about marriage from them?

_____

How did this affect your expectations about relationships?

_____

_____

_____

Attitude Changes You'd Like to Make Regarding Relationships

This exercise is designed to help you make some basic changes in your attitudes about relationships. Make a commitment to yourself that you will take the action steps that you say you will within one week after you write down what you want to change.

Examples

1. I would like to be more generous.

    Action step: I will listen to my friend Mary more attentively

    Action step: I will take out the garbage without being asked.

2. I would like to be more assertive.

    Action step: I will tell Jack that I was hurt by his remark yesterday.

    Action step: I will tell my mother that I am too busy to attend her brunch next Sunday.

Now it's your turn.

1. _____

    Action step: _____

    Action step: _____

2. _____

    Action step: _____

    Action step: _____

3. _____

    Action step: _____

    Action step: _____

4. _____

    Action step: _____

    Action step: _____

5. _____

     Action step: _____

     Action step: _____

Stop Selling Yourself Short—Learn to Acknowledge Your Strengths

Your greatest obstacle to achieving a healthy balanced relationship may be an unconscious pattern of minimizing your own gifts and talents. If your childhood was marked by severe criticisms, judgments, or neglect, you may have learned to focus on your liabilities rather than your assets.

The following exercise will help you to shine the light on your strengths and to build your self- esteem. When you feel good about who you are, you are most able to attract the partner you truly desire.

Exercise: Your Top Ten List

List ten reasons someone would be happy to be in a relationship with you.

Examples

I am a kind and sensitive person . . . I am playful . . . I am attractive . . . I am health conscious . . . I am funny . . . I have a great smile . . . I am a gentle soul . . . I am a good athlete . . . I am a great cook . . . I play great guitar . . . I am a good teacher . . . I am intelligent . . .

1. _____

2. _____

3. _____

4. _____

5. _____

6. _____

7. _____

8. _____

9. _____

10. _____

Facing Your Fears of Being Close

The same fence that shuts others out shuts you in.

—Bill Copeland

If you have been injured through abandonment, exposure, or engulfment, your mind builds an assortment of defensive strategies (usually unconsciously) that will attempt to prevent you from ever getting hurt again. These forms of self-protection become "hard-wired" into your mental computer and are acted out with the people in your life.

The process of "working through" these defenses requires that you acknowledge that they are there. Yet seeing your defenses can be very difficult because, most likely, they have become blindspots. The task can be made easier if someone you trust points out what those blindspots are.

Therapist:	Have you ever noticed that every time I bring up the sadness I see in your eyes, you change the subject?
Bob:	I didn't realize that. I guess I believe that people will call you weak if you show you are hurt. My father always did.
Therapist:	I noticed that in group therapy you rarely ask for time. I wonder if you are minimizing your self-importance to protect yourself in some way?
Jane:	I guess I protect myself that way from people thinking I'm not very smart. After all, a lot of what I have to say doesn't seem very important.
Therapist:	I noticed that when you talk about relationship struggles, you have this tendency to analyze and intellectualize the situation. I wonder how you feel?
Fred:	Really? I thought I explained how I felt. I guess it's hard to identify my feelings.
Therapist:	I've noticed that it is very difficult for you to ask for help. I wonder what that is about?
Jackie:	My experience is that people will always let you down. I feel safer just doing everything myself.
Therapist:	I notice that every time you start to talk about your pain, you get angry and start criticizing someone.
Frank:	I didn't realize that. I guess it's my way of staying in control and keeping people from criticizing people like my dad always did.

Your psychological defenses are adaptive solutions from your past. They helped you survive when you were a child. And you still try to use them to protect you from further injury. However, they can become ingrained in your way of seeing and managing relationships. It is imperative that you learn to distinguish when these defenses are still needed and when they are actually keeping you from being happy.

Working Through the Fears of Intimacy

The secret of love is in opening up your heart. It's okay to feel afraid, but don't let it stand in your way. Everyone knows that love is the only road.

—James Taylor

Exercise: Four Steps to Breaking Free

Step 1: List five ways you were abandoned (left), engulfed (smothered), or exposed (shamed) emotionally or physically when you were a child.

Examples

My father often promised to spend time with me on weekends, but he usually ended up staying at the office.

My mother would become cold, distant, and withdrawn every time I disagreed with her.

My father left home when I was five and never came back.

My stepmother would send me to my room every time I expressed my feelings.

My brother would walk away every time I beat him at any game.

1. _____
2. _____
3. _____
4. _____
5. _____

Step 2: List five ways that describe how you protect yourself (the decisions you made about men/women).

Examples

I stopped being honest with my mother.

I did anything I could to avoid conflict.

I stopped trusting my father and most authority figures.

I stuffed my feelings and stayed quietly resentful.

I never allowed myself to get emotionally close to anyone.

1. _____
2. _____
3. _____

4. _____

5. _____

Step 3: How does this protection set you up for loneliness and dissatisfaction today?

Examples

When I stopped being honest with people and became resentful, I pushed people away from me and they eventually gave up on me.

When I became a caretaker I wouldn't allow people to give to me. They never felt very close and eventually pulled away too.

1. _____

2. _____

3. _____

4. _____

5. _____

Step 4: New choices you can make.

Examples

I can start to see how I am repeating the past by distancing others.

I can learn to take small risks with people to see if they will in fact abandon or reject me.

1. _____

2. _____

3. _____

4. _____

5. _____

Creating Love: Ways to Enhance Love in Your Life

> *The meeting of two personalities is like the contact of two chemical substances: if there is a reaction, both are transformed.*
>
> —C. G. Jung

Love is a choice. There are some people who quietly wait for an overwhelming flood of emotion to decide they are experiencing love. Although this kind of overwhelming

emotion can appear at times, it is the *intention* of experiencing and creating love that will bring it to your life on a regular basis. You can make the choice to think loving thoughts, share loving feelings, and act in loving ways.

Several times each day, repeat the following sentence to yourself:

"I deserve love. I want love in my life. I am willing to create love through loving actions on a daily basis."

Here are some ways you can share your loving feelings:

- Listen to others and reflect back what you hear

- Acknowledge another's strengths

- Give someone a hug

- Surprise someone with a gift

- Remember a birthday

- Surprise someone with a bundle of balloons

- Plan an adventure day to a scenic location

- Wash the dishes

- Write an unexpected love note

Give all to love; obey the heart.

—Ralph Waldo Emerson

Positive Things You Can Say to Yourself

- Relationships are wonderful opportunities to heal the pain of the past and open up to love and acceptance in the present.

- I am completely responsible for my words and actions. I choose to create love rather than to recycle hurt and anger.

- Both my partner and I can have what we want in this relationship if we work together, listen carefully to each other, express our needs, and support one another.

- Telling the truth in an assertive (not aggressive) way will allow a relationship to grow and will create greater intimacy.

- When I find fault with others I should first try to understand what this says about me.

- I have the right to ask for what I want and need.

- A healthy relationship allows for intimate times together and space for time alone.

- I have the right to say no to requests I do not want to meet.

- I accept my partner's and my own limitations as an opportunity to practice love and acceptance.

- Relationships are meant to be fun, nurturing, and fulfilling, but they will not be that way every moment of the day.

- It's more important to be happy than to be right.

- I am completely responsible for my words and actions. I choose to speak lovingly rather than with judgment or indifference.

- Love is a verb, not a noun. I will create more love in my world today by thinking about what's good about my relationships and sharing these thoughts.

Positive Things You Can Do for Yourself

- Take time for yourself when you need it.

- Spend at least forty-five minutes of quality time each day with your significant other.

- Move slowly into a new relationship, take time to get to know this person. Get information. Listen to your instincts.

- Be the person you are, not the one others want you to be.

- Be clear about expressing what you want and don't want.

- Cultivate connections with people who have a lot in common with you.

- Keep a feelings journal. Be careful about collecting unexpressed resentments.

- Listen without giving advice unless you are asked for it.

- Create regular time to acknowledge your partner. Bring her/him unexpected gifts.

- Develop a support system of friends rather than keeping all your emotional eggs in one basket.

When You Can't Find Meaning in Your Life

*The Sixth Key: Purpose—
Getting in Touch with What
Is Truly Meaningful to You and
Learning to Bring It to Life*

Understanding the Key Issue

"When I was pregnant with Adrianna, and I felt her move inside of me for the first time, everything I was stressed out about instantly seemed small and silly. Here was the important thing. Here was what really mattered.

"I don't think anything can take the place of those years when you're raising your kids. You're tying shoelaces, trying to get your baby to drink from a cup instead of a bottle, watching soccer practice, sitting next to your teenager as she drives your car for the first time, shopping for a dress for the prom. You always have a purpose. Then, if you do this well, they go off on their own. And if you're lucky—and I do feel lucky—they call

you from college or visit you with their fiancée and you plan a wedding and you walk down an aisle in front of all of your friends. But this child that was so much a part of your life is no longer all yours anymore.

"My friends say, 'What a relief it must be to know you raised a daughter and she's so happy with her own life. Now you've got time to do what you want to do.' But what do I want to do? I never gave it any thought, and I was too busy to think most of the time. I don't want to be a mother who lives for the phone calls. I don't want to guilt-trip a daughter who is exactly what I hoped she'd be, even though she now lives a thousand miles away from me. I have time to decide what I want to do with the rest of my life. But I don't even know how to go about such a task. Think about myself? What do I want? I have no experience thinking about that. I've had too many years keeping busy worrying about everyone else."

Here is someone else struggling with the same issue. "My grandfather was a lawyer. My father is a lawyer. I have two brothers. I'm the youngest. All three of us are lawyers. I'm a tax lawyer. My father said this was the way to go. He was constantly pointing out how my brother who became a public defender was always exhausted by too many responsibilities and not having enough cash.

"I feel an emptiness about my entire career. But my wife gets upset when I talk about changing careers. She's got a lot invested in being a lawyer's wife, and I don't blame her. She sees the mortgage, credit card bills, the membership at the country club where my kids swim, and my wife and I both golf there with friends we've made over the years. I've got two young kids who need to be in private school if we're going to continue to live in Manhattan. I'd like to hear someone tell me how I can get off this treadmill without jeopardizing everything I've worked so hard for."

Do you experience similar struggles? The following quiz can help you determine whether what's missing in your life is a sense of purpose.

Do You Feel Your Life Has Purpose?

Questionnaire

Read each statement and put a checkmark in the appropriate box (0 = never, 1 = sometimes, 2 = always).

Does your life have purpose?	0	1	2	3
1. I feel my daily activities are meaningful.				
2. I believe that what I do (e.g., raising children, my career, my activities) is important.				
3. I feel like I contribute to others.				
4. I feel I have a purpose that guides my choices in life.				

5. I rarely feel empty or lost.				
6. I feel I am on the earth for a purpose.				
7. I have an active spiritual life.				
8. I share my passions and deepest feelings with others.				
9. I feel I am a valuable person with a lot to give.				
10. I often contemplate what is meaningful for me and I change my goals accordingly.				

Scoring

For each "always" give yourself two points. Give yourself 1 point for each "sometimes" and no points for each "never."

Your total score: _____

Here's how to interpret your score.

15–20: You value meaning and purpose in your life and you strive to find it. You feel that your life has direction and you usually can see the bigger picture.

10–14: You struggle at times to find meaning in your life or to stay on track with what you feel your true purpose is. You can get caught up in details or stray off the path you would rather be on. Working with this chapter will help bring your purpose back into focus.

9 or less: Finding meaning and purpose in your life is something you struggle with. Sometimes you probably wonder, "What's it all for?" The exercises in this chapter may help you discover some basics that will help you answer that question in a way that's meaningful for you.

Discovering the Root of Your Struggles

Many spiritual leaders teach that each of us comes into the world to learn and to accomplish certain things. When we are in synch with that purpose we are closest to fulfillment. Sometimes we have a sense of that purpose. Sometimes we lose sight of it. Sometimes we are completely unaware of what our purpose is.

When we struggle to find meaning in our lives and it continues to elude us, the chances are good that's because of one of the following reasons:

- Feeling a sense of scarcity rather than a sense of abundance

- Having grown up in a family that groomed you for a lifestyle that's not what you would have chosen for yourself

- Feeling a lack of empathy, validation, and support (see chapter 3)

- Having a fear of looking within

Let's look more closely at each of these.

A Sense of Scarcity versus a Sense of Abundance

We have clients with very small or inconsistent incomes who feel financially secure. As one client put it, "I know, no matter what happens, I'll land on my feet." They aren't careless or impractical, either. These people have a deep belief that there is enough to go around, they have a natural sense of abundance.

We also have clients who have large incomes and many investments who are fearful every moment of not having enough money. For the person who lives with such a sense of scarcity, there is truly never enough. Therefore, he or she is much more apt to go for the sure thing, the instant payoff, the action that will pay the bills today, than to take the type of risks involved in seeking a higher purpose or meaning in life.

Karla, thirty-five, is a case in point. She is a special education teacher who works with severely learning disabled children. "Every so often I'll meet someone and they'll ask me what I do, and when I tell them, they'll say something like, 'Oh, you're such a special person to work with those children. It must be so rewarding.' I really want to die when they say that. I got my degree in special education simply because that's where the jobs were, and I knew that I had to have a job the day I graduated from college or I'd have no way to survive. To be honest, my job is boring and tedious. To me, there's nothing meaningful about it at all. I know that there were probably other things I could have done with my life that I might have enjoyed more. But, hey, with a mortgage, a divorce, and a teenager, I was too afraid to go for it."

A sense of scarcity is like a filter through which we view everything. It's not necessarily reality. However, it is a way to protect ourselves from risk and disappointment. In truth, it often limits us to a life that is somewhere in the middle between happiness and unhappiness. It's usually steady and stable. "I guess I'd call it vanilla," Karla says. "It's not a sundae with all the trimmings, but at least you're eating ice cream." You might think Karla is being practical. But thirteen years doing a job she dislikes goes beyond practicality. It's her enduring sense of scarcity that won't allow her to see that she does, in fact, have other options.

Where do you stand on the scarcity versus abundance continuum? Answer the following questions as either true or false.

	T	F
1. I often worry that there won't be enough money even when things are going well.		
2. In choosing a career, security is a top priority.		

3. I often worry about losing what I've gained through no fault of my own.		
4. I rarely take risks with things that are dearest to me.		
5. I have trouble believing the saying, "Do what you love and the money will follow."		
6. I worry that my children won't have as many opportunities in their lives as earlier generations before them had.		
7. I have trouble believing that eventually everything works out.		
8. I don't feel especially connected to anything beyond my day-to-day activities.		
9. When people say, "Don't worry, it will work out," I think they're naïve.		
10. I have doubts whether there is a Higher Power who has a master plan for me.		
11. When I leave a relationship, it's usually because I've met someone else. I'd rather stay in an unsatisfying relationship than be alone.		
12. Making changes in my life, whether it means moving to another home, or switching careers, can be very difficult for me.		

Scoring

Have you answered "true" more often than "false"? That doesn't mean you're right or wrong. When you see scarcity all around you, just remember that taking the time to pursue questions like "What would have real meaning for me? What do I really want?" becomes more difficult. Asking such questions may seem impractical, but that doesn't mean it is impractical. This isn't an either/or type of endeavor, where you either take wild risks or stay stuck with what you have. There are ways you can begin to feel a greater, more freeing sense of abundance in your life without having to give up the tried and true.

Family Grooming

John's story: "There was no question that I was going to go into the family business. I knew that almost from the moment I could walk."

Martha's story: "Marry a businessman with prospects, work for a year, then have your first child and move to the suburbs. That's what my mother always told me to do; I never even thought to question it."

Harry's story: "I was good at fixing things, I loved building things. I probably would have enjoyed a job in construction, or remodeling homes, or anything working with my hands. But my parents wouldn't hear of anything except college and a business major."

You might ask, "Why didn't these people just stand up to their parents?" Well, actually, it was only in retrospect that they discovered their lives had been chosen for them.

What their parents told them to do seemed to make sense at the time. When it didn't add up to happiness and fulfillment, they were genuinely surprised and confused. When your family predestines you for a lifestyle that's not your true calling, it is not surprising that you may be successful, but not feel that your life has any purpose or meaning.

Call it a rite of passage, a midlife crisis, or a spiritual awakening, but whatever name you give it, most of us arrive at a time in our lives when we begin to question everything we do and what meaning it has. Those of us who followed a path laid out for us by someone else sometimes begin to feel angry or ashamed. Did we just take the easy way out? Were we pushed too hard into places we didn't want to go? Maybe so. But it isn't too late. Awareness is the first step. It doesn't matter so much how you got on the path you're on. What matters is whether you feel fulfilled or empty.

Fear of Looking Within

For some of you, questions such as, "What do you really want to accomplish with your life?" or "What do you feel your true purpose is?" are overwhelming. You can be afraid to look inside yourself for many reasons. First, if you don't know the answers to such questions, you can become confused or frustrated and then want to avoid the entire process of introspection.

Second, you may be afraid of upsetting someone else's values, such as your parents or even your friends. Twenty-five-year-old Tom, for example, researched graduate schools for two years and has more than fifty catalogs and blank application forms. "The catalogs were gathering dust because I could never make a decision about what program to follow. At least, that's what I thought. The truth is I am afraid to face my father and say, 'Dad, thanks for the offer to put me through an MBA program, but I don't really want work to be the focus of my life. I want to have a more balanced life.' You say something like that to him and he'll think you're from another planet. It's very difficult for me to concentrate on what *I* want, because my father keeps telling me what to do. I think of my father's bewildered face; his disappointment that his son won't have the same kind of success that he's had, and I thank God that I met a woman who encourages me to think for myself. But it's still difficult to separate what I want from my father's values."

Furthermore, you may suspect that answering questions about your purpose, or what would be meaningful to you, would mean you would have to make many changes in your life, and that can be scary in itself. One client told us of her earlier therapy, years ago, when her therapist asked her, "What do you really want from a relationship?" She said to us, "I was in therapy because I was depressed, but I didn't want to look at my marriage at all. I wouldn't even answer the question. I knew it would be like opening Pandora's box. I wasn't ready to face how meaningless our relationship had become because then I knew I'd have to do something about it." Years later, she was feeling stronger and was more willing to delve into her personal needs and desires, even if it meant taking a hard look at her marriage.

If exploring yourself to find your true purpose means that much of the foundation upon which you've built your life is shaky and must be replaced, some of you will avoid doing it. You need to have enough support to feel strong enough to cope with the answer.

The Lack of Empathy, Validation, and Support

Kyle was walking down the beach with his wife on a beautiful day. He started to whistle and then he grabbed his wife's hand and said, "Listen to this. I have a great idea for an advertising jingle. I've got to run this by my brother." He started to hum it, then he put a rhyme to it and laughed out loud because it was so funny and clever. Halfway through he looked at his wife. She was looking out at the beach, barely listening. Kyle knew what she was thinking, because he was thinking the same thing: His brother was a vice president at one of the top advertising firms in the country, heading a team of people who did nothing but create prize-winning slogans and catchy tunes for a living. Why in the world should he listen to his little brother's jingle?

"I immediately started to feel depressed and angry. I was thinking, 'You never support me. I'm not going to talk to you about this stuff again. I'll find someone else who appreciates this.'"

Many of us received this kind of response when we were young. Our parents told us to be practical. "Stop drawing in class, and pay attention to the teacher!" Or "Your math scores are so high, what do you mean you don't want to major in math?"

Make no mistake about this. It takes support and validation to take a dream or an idea and run with it into unfamiliar territory. Without support, it's easy to blame other people as the reason why we never followed our dreams and why we're stuck with little meaning in our lives: "She wanted three kids. Now my whole life is one big *should*. I don't have the luxury of doing what I really want to do."

But don't believe that's the end of the story. You might surprise yourself. There are plenty of people whose shoulders are weighted down with responsibility but who still find time to write poetry, coach little league teams in the inner city, take part in community affairs, find a bigger purpose. You need to find support and validation, but you also need to be clear about your goals and not give up the moment validation isn't immediately forthcoming.

If you are fearful about putting aside practicalities to find something more meaningful, so is your spouse. So are many of your friends, which may be one of the reasons why you find the common ground to be friends in the first place. When you become clearer about what you want to have happen in your life, and you begin to really believe it can happen, your enthusiasm may win over the people who are not supportive. If not, perhaps you are the person who, by example, teaches everyone around you that there is a bigger, more meaningful picture. That, in itself, may be your highest purpose.

Rx: Finding Out What Is Meaningful for You.

*Cherish your visions and your dreams as they are the children
of your soul; the blueprints of your ultimate achievements.*

—Napoleon Hill

Your Key Questions

1. What do you love to do? When do you feel the most satisfaction?
   (E.g., *making things beautiful; playing the piano; working in my studio; teaching, designing things on the computer.*)

   _____

   _____

   _____

   _____

   _____

2. How could your gifts and talents fulfill a need in the world?
   (E.g., *my art skills could bring joy to elderly people; my teaching skills could educate children; my optimism could motivate others.*)

   _____

   _____

   _____

   _____

   _____

3. What would you like people to say about you after you're gone?
   (E.g., *he/she was a good person; creative, loving, talented; enjoyed life to the fullest.*)

   _____

   _____

_____

_____

_____

_____

4. In what ways would you act differently if you had only one year to live?
   (E.g., *make sure I made a contribution to what I believe in; tell people I love how I feel about them; visit places I've always wanted to see.*)

_____

_____

_____

_____

_____

See How Your Symptoms Serve You

When you have bills to pay and responsibilities to discharge, of course it makes sense to go to work tomorrow morning rather than to sit and ponder your purpose in life. No, you can't just abandon the two-year-old who needs you because you feel that potty-training isn't your higher purpose. But when it seems as if you can do only one and not the other, you need to take a closer look at the payoffs you receive for allowing your higher purpose to wait indefinitely in the wings.

Symptom	Protective Function
1. Playing it safe	1. Security; avoid conflict; protection from failure; avoid rejection; staying with the familiar rather than the challenging.
2. Bored and restless	2. Protection from risk; management of anxiety.
3. Feeling empty	3. Retreat from feelings; excuse to give up.
4. Finding flaws with your plan to change your life and make it more meaningful	4. Excuse to give up; beat others to the punch.

Creating New Choices

Choose one to three examples of not following through on meaningful activities in your life that you believe are currently causing frustration. Then complete the chart below.

- In the first column, write one to three activities that you would find meaningful and enjoyable.

- In the second column , write the protective function of not following through.

- In the third column, write the downside to this solution.

- In the fourth column, write a more effective solution to this problem.

Example

Activity	Protective Function of Not Following Through	Downside to This Solution	New Choices
I'd like to volunteer to coach softball but I don't because I keep thinking "Why spend the time when you don't make the money."	Fear of taking on a commitment without an assured payoff. Avoiding the possibility that they may not like me or I wouldn't be very good at this.	I'd like to work with kids, I'm a good coach and I need the exercise. I could really benefit from some new activities with kids, especially since I don't have any of my own.	I could go watch some games. I could participate without committing to full-time coaching and see how it feels.

Now it's your turn.

Activity	Protective Function of Not Following Through	Downside to This Solution	New Choices
1.			
2.			

3.			

Clarifying Your Purpose

Whether you know it or not, your sense of purpose is already there. Perhaps you grew up in an environment where your true self was denied. Your parents had their agendas set up for you. Maybe they were too absorbed in their own problems to pay attention to yours. Whatever the reason, you can start to listen to yourself now.

Each one of us has a unique talent and a unique way of expressing that talent. Put another way, there is something each one of us can do better than anyone else. What are your unique gifts?

Sean, forty-six, a recording engineer, tells the story of finding out what his unique gifts were and describes his life transition from despair to purpose:

"I worked in the same job as a recording engineer for years. My work was to record the music that my clients had written. There were long periods of time when I just sat around waiting for the producer to pull all the pieces together. My job was mainly to turn knobs. 'Hey, Sean! Roll off the bass. Boost the highs.' I spent most of my time waiting for instructions, sometimes for hours and hours.

"Although my clients were extremely creative writers, the environment was tense. To keep my job, a pleasant attitude was a requirement. Each year I felt more frustration and tension. I was becoming very depressed.

"The work itself was worse than the tension or the waiting. I wasn't happy just polishing other people's work, being just a tool that someone else used in creating their own work. My work had become boring and repetitive. There was nowhere to go and no way to grow. I felt as if I was on a treadmill to Hell. I had lost the sense of who I was. I used to feel I was a creative and positive person who worked in the music business. It sounded great on paper but it had no meaning for me. I became more and more angry, frustrated, and bad-tempered. I didn't know who I was anymore and I was afraid I wasn't going to get myself back.

"The turning point came when I realized there *was* something that I loved to do. I became passionate about computers, the Macintosh especially. One day I bought a little laptop. I began to use all the time that I had previously wasted at the studio. I started working on the computer and I developed new skills. I learned a new database language. I used my downtime to get proficient at computing. Suddenly, I started looking forward to having nothing to do at work. Waiting time became creative time. Instead of driving to work I started taking the train so that I could do some work while I commuted, as well. I got really fired up. I felt motivated. I began to think that there might be a way to do something I really liked a lot.

"My transition from sound engineer to computer programmer wasn't quick. But it was so much more meaningful. I learned that I can be a creator. As an engineer, I was always working with someone else's project. As a computer programmer, I *create* a pro-

gram that does something that I want it to do, in the way I want it to do it. It looks the way I want it to look. When I am done with it, I can show it to someone and say, 'I made this.' It's a totally different feeling.

"The shift to becoming a creator was really tough, because I had always seen myself as an enabler. I thought my basic skill was helping other people to accomplish their work. It took courage to dig down and discover that I can also be an originator.

"Now, I think I am on a more honest path, one where I express myself more completely. I have a statement of purpose that I've programmed into a multicolored screensaver on my computer. It reads, 'I am a joyful creator openly sharing myself and my talents with others for the benefit of all concerned.'"

Making the kind of transition that Sean made isn't easy and it's seldom quick. But it's so much more rewarding than obsessing about an unfulfilling job. If you want to move forward on a new career path, one of the most helpful places to start is to design your own personal mission statement. To help you design your personal mission statement answer the following questions as quickly as you can. Write the first things that come to mind. This will honor your intuition and perhaps enable you to sidestep your inner critic.

Your Statement of Purpose

What things in my life are most important to me?
(E.g., *family, personal growth, music, nature, sports, pleasure, relationships.*)

_____

_____

_____

_____

_____

_____

What would I like to contribute to the world?
(E.g., *creativity, music, inspiration, books, healing, playfulness.*)

_____

_____

_____

_____

_____

_____

In this lifetime, I hope to ...
(E.g., *live each day fully; spread joy; teach children; have fun; connect deeply with others.*)

_____

_____

_____

_____

_____

How can I make these things happen in my life?
(E.g., *I can live each day consciously; follow a list of personal goals; share my dreams with others.*)

_____

_____

_____

_____

_____

Who are the people can I work with on this journey?
(E.g., *my parents, siblings, friends, teachers, co-workers.*)

_____

_____

_____

_____

_____

Now look at your answers to the above questions and consolidate them into a statement of purpose.

My Statement of Purpose

Example

My purpose is to live each day fully and creatively. To build lasting friendships that are based on fun, mutual support, and common interests. To leave a legacy of memories, books, and music that will bring joy and inspiration to others.

Now it's your turn.

_____

_____

_____

_____

_____

Disputing Your Self-Defeating Thoughts

It's easy to say some dream or aspiration that has special meaning for you is silly, impractical, or impossible. You need to learn what to say to your inner critic when that voice chimes in with negative messages about how you are wasting your time.

Exercise

1. Think of something you would like to do if it was failsafe, that is, if you couldn't fail. (E.g., *I would like write a short story and get it published*.)

2. What are the thoughts that make you back off? The thoughts that stop you before you begin.

   - I'm not a good enough writer.

   - I don't have the credentials.

   - The whole idea is silly.

   - When would I have the time to do this?

3. Now answer each of these thoughts with a more empowering response.

I'm not a good enough writer.

_____

_____

I got good grades in writing in school. How will I know until I try? I can take a writing class to refine my skills.

_____

_____

I don't have the credentials.

_____

_____

Many published authors do not have degrees in writing. Look at John Grisham. He was a lawyer.

_____

_____

When would I have the time to do this?

_____

_____

I spend hours on the weekends watching TV or just puttering around. I'm sure I could make the time.

_____

_____

This idea is silly.

_____

_____

The beanie baby was a silly idea, but look what happened. Beanie babies became a national craze.

_____

_____

Waking Up to the Present

> *Don't it always seem to go, you don't know what you got till it's gone. They paved paradise and put up a parking lot.*

> —Joni Mitchell

If you knew that everything in your life was going to end tomorrow, you'd probably live much more purposefully today. This is the essence of the Buddhist notion of impermanence.

In his book *Thoughts Without a Thinker* (1995) psychiatrist Mark Epstein describes an encounter in a Laotian forest monastery with a famous master, Achaan Chaa, which made an indelible impression on a group of American travelers.

"You see this goblet?' Chaa asked, holding up a glass. "For me, this glass is already broken. I enjoy it; I drink out of it. It holds my water admirably, sometimes even reflecting the sun in beautiful patterns. If I should tap it, it has a lovely ring to it. But when I put this glass on a shelf and the wind knocks it over or my elbow brushes it off the table and it falls to the ground and shatters, I say, 'Of course.' When I understand that the glass is already broken, every moment with it is precious."

Exercise: Impermanence

1. Close your eyes and visualize someone or something that is very precious to you. Spend a few moments seeing this picture in vivid detail.

2. Now, imagine this person or thing gone forever. Really see this as if it had happened. Pay attention to your thoughts and feelings.

3. Now write about your experience.

_____

_____

_____

_____

_____

_____

Spirituality in Everyday Life

> *I think we would be able to live in this world more peaceably if our spirituality were to come from not just looking into infinity but very closely at the world around us—and appreciating its depth and divinity.*
>
> —Thomas Moore

Many people have grown up with a cynical view of spirituality. Yet this disconnection with anything larger than ourselves can create an emptiness and isolation in our lives. Spirituality can look different to different people. For some, it's a walk in the woods, to

others it's meditation or music, and to some it's going to church. You can find a spiritual connection that is right for you.

How does spirituality show itself in everyday life? Here are some answers we received to this question from friends, colleagues, and clients.

- Having a deep meaningful conversation with a close friend

- Watching a sunset

- Listening to music

- Arranging a bouquet of flowers

- Paying attention to the present moment

- Being present during a birth

- Playing with a pet

- Meditating

- Hiking in the mountains

- Exercising

- Going to a house of worship and taking part in the service

- Singing

- Looking at the stars

- Helping others

- Having compassion for our shortcomings

What Does Spirituality Mean to You?

_____

_____

_____

_____

_____

_____

We are not human beings trying to be spiritual.
We are spiritual beings trying to be human.

—Jacquelyn Small

The Spiritual Shift from "What's in This for Me"? to "How Can I Be of Help to Others?"

There are two ways of spreading light; to be
the candle or the mirror that reflects it.

—Edith Wharton

So many of us grew up in a climate of scarcity. Perhaps there wasn't enough food on the table or clothes in the closet. Or perhaps we craved parental attention that we never got. When we come from a background of scarcity, many of us never feel there is enough—even if there is plenty. Our fear compels us to think, "What about me?" or "What's in this for me?" We have trouble giving to others. Or perhaps you grew up in a family that catered to your every need. In this case, you may have developed a sense of entitlement, expecting the world to cater to you. You will also have trouble giving to others.

However your history may have shaped you, you are missing one of the most purposeful experiences in life—the experience of contributing. The following exercise will help you shift your ego-based thought of "What's in this for me?" to the spiritual perspective of contributing.

How Giving Are You?

Choose the answer that sounds the most like you.

1. Your neighbor is frantic because she has to take an unexpected business trip and she needs someone to feed her four cats and scoop the litter for the next two days. When she asks you for help you think

    a. This woman calls me only when she needs something. What does she ever do for me? Too bad about her cats.

    b. I'll tell her I'll do it if she absolutely can't find anyone else.

    c. No big deal to pour a little cat food into a dish, scoop some litter, and make sure none of the cats is trapped in a closet or something. I'm glad I can help her out.

2. You're stopped at a red light and a man is walking around the intersection from car to car, asking for money to help inner city kids. You think

a. I hate these people who make up stories about inner city kids to make people feel guilty, and then they use the money to buy alcohol.

b. I'd give him some money, but once you start there is no end to it—homeless people, men selling newspapers, women begging on the corner. When is enough, enough?

c. If I give him a dollar, what's the big deal?

3. It's the Christmas season, and your department is throwing a bash to celebrate. A sign-up list is circulating the office—can you bring a salad, a main dish, or a dessert? You think

a. Why doesn't the company throw a dinner at a restaurant downtown to congratulate us for all the work we have done? This bring-your-own-food party is another travesty of meaningful employment, and one more reason why I hate this company.

b. I'll see my friends, the party will be fun, but I'm not going to conjure up any gourmet dishes here. I'll pick up a few vats of potato salad at the deli and that will be my contribution.

c. Great chance to have people sample my broccoli casserole. I might even bring a shrimp appetizer.

4. You send your neighbors an expensive bottle of wine the day they move into their new house as a welcome-to-the-neighborhood gift. The husband says thanks when you cross paths on the way to your cars a week later. The wife never says a word. You think

a. What jerks. They could have at least sent a thank-you note. I should have sent a cheaper bottle of wine.

b. He's okay, but I don't ever want anything to do with her.

c. They must be absolutely crazed after such a big move. I hope they enjoyed the wine.

5. You've been coaching the Little League, and it's something you love to do, especially because you think it gets your son out in the open air, away from his computer games. This year your son tells you that he absolutely doesn't want to be on the team anymore and he won't budge. What happens to your coaching? You think

a. Goodbye Little League. Why bother if my son is not on the team?

b. I'll give up coaching, but still make as many games as I can and help where I can, but without my son on the team, I think it will end up being too much hassle.

   c. I'm the coach. I'm needed. My son's decisions are his own, but I'm still going to be there this season to carry on.

6. How often do you feel that you give a lot more to people than you get back?

   a. All the time. I deeply resent being used.

   b. Some of the time, with some of the people I'm close to who seem to take me for granted. I like to help people out, but I think relationships should be 50/50 and I don't want to be used.

   c. Not often, because I don't really think about what I'm going to get back. I like the idea of helping someone out, regardless of what I get back.

7. When it comes to weddings, baby showers, engagement parties, you feel

   a. Overwhelmed. These invitations to these celebrations cost major money for people you're not even close to, and don't really care about.

   b. Aggravated, but hey, these people came to your kid's bar mitzvah, so you've got to go to their kid's bar mitzvah, and maybe it will be fun.

   c. Excited. You're the first one in the house with a casserole, a bouquet of flowers, or a hug.

8. Your best friend talks to you about his/her need to make a contribution—to give something back to society. You think

   a. Midlife crisis! He's probably having trouble with his wife. This sudden New Age thinking makes me wonder whether he's having an affair.

   b. I agree. But isn't holding down a full-time job, raising kids, and helping aging parents a contribution?

   c. Me too. How can we do this together?

9. When you hear the old saying, "To give is to receive," you think

   a. On what planet?

   b. Well, it depends on who you give to.

   c. Absolutely true. You can always make a difference, even if it's not immediate.

10. How do you feel about loaning someone your bicycle?

   a. Never. Too much risk.

   b. Depends. If it's not a new bike and I trust the person, I'd do it.

   c. I do it all the time.

Scoring

It probably wasn't hard for you to see that the "a" answers are the answers of the skeptic, who has reservations about giving and often feels taken advantage of. If this is you, it is important to realize that being skeptical about being a giver does not make you a bad person and there are probably excellent reasons why you feel the way you do.

If all your answers are "c's" it is obvious that giving comes easily to you. However, you could be giving much more than you receive, and end up just as dissatisfied with your life as the person who never gives at all. A combination of "b" and "c" answers indicates balance in the area of giving and receiving between a desire to contribute to others and a healthy sense of your own needs. If you want to increase your giving and contributing to others, here are some simple ways to do that:

This week find five ways you can contribute something to others. Make it simple. Give up your seat on the bus to someone who is standing. Smile at a stranger. Help someone carry their groceries. Compliment someone.

Mindfulness: Learning to Live in the Present

> *The ordinary arts we practice every day at home are of more importance to the soul than their simplicity might suggest.*
>
> —Thomas Moore

Many of us have a hard time staying focused on our purpose because we are too distracted by other things. Joan Borysenko in *Minding the Body, Mending the Mind* (1987, 89) writes: "If you could train your mind to let go of other desires, returning to them when the actual moment has come to do the bills and make the phone call, you would be able to experience peace of mind. The road to peace of mind is through a practice called mindfulness."

A recent seminar on "mindfulness" was packed, with standing room only. The participants were there to learn to stop worrying about what might have been or what could be. They wanted to be here now, totally in the present. An hour into the program, the seminar leader passed out oranges with the following instructions: "Look at the orange. See the colors. Feel and taste the orange. Concentrate."

Staring at their oranges for ten minutes, half of the people in the room were thinking, "How much longer until we break for lunch? I feel so stupid doing this." Or even, "How is this going to help me make more money?"

What's the real intent of this exercise and how would you benefit from really concentrating on that orange? You'd taste the orange more fully. You'd use all of your senses. You'd clear your mind of all other thoughts and purposes and focus on a single experience. Perhaps you would notice something or experience something you never had before. Yes, it's only an orange. But have you ever bathed your kids while munching a quick

sandwich and talking on the phone to a friend while the news is blaring on the TV in the background? You'd miss all the joy of bathing a child and the sudsy, slippery fun that bath time can be. You'd half hear what your friend is saying and you'd miss the feeling of connection with someone you care for. You wouldn't even taste what you were eating. You would have become what some call a "human doing" instead of a "human being." You would lose sight of the purpose of all of these activities—love, nourishment, friendship, awareness—and end up with the anxieties of a client who told us: "I feel like if I don't keep pushing, pushing, pushing, it'll all fall apart."

Perhaps your worries about the future are what distracts you from experiencing the simple things more fully. A twenty-seven-year-old woman confided, "Sure I worry about the future too much. I don't want to set myself up for disappointment. I want to be on top of problems. The trouble is, lately, I think I'm trading hours of worry to avoid a lot of stuff that never happens."

You may have the illusion that if you keep trying to figure it out, worry about it, obsess about it, you'll reach the answer quicker. That if you learn to do three things at once, you'll ultimately achieve more. Very often, the opposite is true. Creativity is rooted in the ability to focus. Achievement is enhanced by focus and clarity of mind.

The ability to focus on the present is what mindfulness is all about. The concept of mindfulness is centuries old. It's been brought to the fore by the New Age spirituality movement, but it is based mostly on Buddhism, which has a growing membership in the United States today. The practice of mindfulness promises such benefits as increased satisfaction with your life, reduced stress, increased ability to focus, greater capacity for intimacy, and more emotional stability.

What can you do to become more mindful? Realize, first, that although your mind is capable of darting around from one thing to another, it can really hold only one thing in full focus at any given moment. Trying to do several things simultaneously wastes time, creates stress, and ultimately makes you feel less alive and vital.

Choose one activity to be more mindful about. It can be something as routine as shaving or taking a shower. It can be taking a walk or making love. When you do the activity, immerse yourself in it fully. If your mind wanders, expect this. Be observant about where it wanders to. With a nonjudgmental attitude gently guide your mind back to the present experience. Breathe deeply and enjoy the moment. Learn how good focusing can feel.

As renowned Vipassana master Thich Nhat Hanh says, "While washing the dishes one should be completely aware of the fact that one is washing the dishes. At first glance that may seem a little silly: Why put so much stress on a simple thing? But that's precisely the point. The fact that I am standing there washing these bowls is a wondrous reality. I'm being completely myself, following my breath and conscious of my presence and conscious of my thoughts and actions. There's no way I can be tossed around mindlessly like a bottle slapped here and there on the waves" (1976).

If you find it hard to stay focused in the present, you may ask yourself, "Is there something I'm running from? Is there something ahead I need to deal with?" Do you feel you'll lose something if you decide that you will only be here, in this moment, and nowhere else? You might want to decide to deal with those issues squarely, once and for all, and finally let them go. As the saying goes, "It may be better to lose our minds and come to our senses."

> *Look at everything as though you were seeing it for the first*
> *or last time. Then your time on earth will be filled with glory.*
>
> —Betty Smith

Exercise: Mindfulness

In our fast-paced world, many of us are caught up doing multiple tasks at the same time. We think we are being efficient and sometimes we are. Yet as we robotically flip through the channels of our TVs, we find our attention span shortens as does our appreciation of the moment.

Instead of reading the newspaper while you eat or watching TV as you talk to your spouse, spend that time (or the next ten minutes) practicing mindfulness. This means experiencing your environment more fully through your senses. Ask yourself, "What am I hearing? What do I see? What do I smell? What am I feeling? What can I taste?" Just observe what you discover. You don't have to do anything with your observations. Just make them attentively and do not invest any emotions in them. Just pay attention.

New Thoughts and New Actions

> *You are a child of god; your playing small doesn't serve the world.*
>
> —Nelson Mandela

Positive Affirmations You Can Say to Yourself

- Today I will start on the journey to my dreams. I will consult my heart for direction and inspiration. In the process I will come home to my true self.

- It doesn't matter where I'm coming from, it matters where I'm going.

- I have a right to define and develop my unique path in life.

- I can be appreciated for being myself.

- Giving to others is giving to myself.

- I have an important voice, and the right to express it.

- I am a channel for God's work.

- I can have everything I want if I help enough other people get what they want.

- I trust in the process of life. I know that Divine wisdom and guidance will protect me at all times.

Positive Things You Can Do for Yourself

- Spend some time each week exploring nature.

- Buy a guided imagery or meditation tape and see how it works for you.

- Ask a trusted friend what he or she thinks your true calling in life is.

- Visit a church, temple, or spiritual environment of your choice and just experience it.

- Plan some quiet time each day when you can relax or meditate. Remember, you don't have to accomplish anything during this time.

- Work in your garden or walk through a forest. Ponder the connectedness of all living things.

- Write a purpose statement for your life including the things you most value.

- Listen to the voice of your own intuition. Take action on these messages.

- Remember the things you loved to do as a child and then find a way to bring them into your life again.

- Start a support group for the artist within you. Find other purpose seekers and share your thoughts and plans with each other.

8

Creating Change: Getting the Results You Want

Your vision will become clear only when you can look into your own heart.
Who looks outside, dreams; who looks inside, awakes.

—Carl Jung

"Why Is It So Hard to Change?"—The Reality of Resistance

Cindy's Story

Cindy, thirty-two, left her therapy session all smiles, bubbling over with ideas. She'd had a brainstorm that was going to change her insignificant future as a personal trainer in a city already replete with trainers into an exciting adventure. She'd had an idea for creating a unique type of exercise manual and software program.

If there was anyone who appeared to be sufficiently motivated to pull it off, Cindy seemed to be the one. She'd spent months examining her own ambivalence about success. "I always had to perform for my father. We all did. It hurt me more than I knew. I've been trying to send out this *message—I'm not going to perform for anyone ever again to get attention, I'm enough just the way I am.* But the only one getting the point of the message is me. Other people just think, 'Here's a girl who talks a good game, but never really gets past go.'

"For thirty-two years, my life hasn't been my own. But I don't want to do this project to please or impress anyone. I'm not even going to tell my father about it. I want to do it because it's exactly what would have helped me when I first started getting into shape. I looked for something like it and couldn't find it, and I know there must be other folks out there who could use it."

The next week at her therapy appointment she was quieter and moodier than she had been at the last session. But her enthusiasm reappeared when she discussed her idea further. "I'm going to make an outline this week," she said as she left.

When we asked how her project was going a week later, her eyes grew dark. "You know, I'm really not here for career counseling. Can't we talk about something else?" She was clearly angry. Suddenly she said, "My father thinks it's a dumb idea, anyway."

Why had she told her father after vowing not to? Clearly, she'd gone to the same dry well for water in spite of many previous failures at that well and in spite of her wealth of insight. What she hadn't understood was that when you try to change a well-established pattern, there can be an enormous amount of unconscious and even conscious resistance.

Kevin's Story

Kevin was a member of one of our therapy groups. He could discuss personality theory from Freud to Maslow to Adler and beyond in incredible depth. He had read more widely than many Ph.D. candidates preparing literature reviews for their dissertations. He was so insightful about other people's problems that his sharp analyses sometimes brought the conversation of half a dozen people to a complete stop as they pondered, "Wow, that's brilliant. That sums the issue up really well." Still, the other group members' nickname for Kevin was "Mr. Yeah-But." When it was his turn to confront his own issues, it often went like this:

Group: Have you thought of calling a friend to talk to when you feel so depressed?

Kevin: Yeah, but I end up feeling worse afterwards, like I'm wallowing in my problems instead of moving forward.

Group: Have you tried to break your goal down into parts, so you won't feel so overwhelmed?

Kevin: Yeah, I have a to-do list. But I never do it.

Group: Maybe you should call one of us when you feel so stuck.

Kevin: Yeah, but when I call you guys at work, I end up in this whole shame thing about why I'm not working, and why I haven't found a new job yet.

Group: This sounds like your same old stuff with your mother.

Kevin: Listen, she's been dead since '79. Why blame her?

After a considerable amount of time taken up by Kevin's "Yeah, buts . . .", everyone in the room was bored. Some tried to hide it. Others looked pointedly at their watches and sent invisible hate-bombs at the therapists for letting Kevin talk so long. They resented Kevin for making them relive what life is like in "The Land of the Forever Stuck."

It may seem strange, but for Kevin, this was a big moment. Everyone had tried to help and everyone had failed. He felt vindicated when the group moved on to the next person. Here were all of these smart people, and no one could help him.

Alana's Story

Alana's type of resistance can be best summed up in the sentence: "I'm too fragile, don't push me." She had many reasons to feel fragile. As a child, she had experienced a great deal of loss. Her only surviving parent was her stepmother. She had become so frustrated with her lack of success at college that she'd been tested by an educational therapist. She was shocked to find that she had tested in the superior range verbally, but was significantly below average in performance. The therapist gave her a list of suggestions to improve her performance and close the gap. She hadn't followed through on any of them.

Like many people, Alana wanted to change her behavior patterns, and knew that change would be the best direction for her to take, but she felt too tired, too depressed, and too vulnerable to take the necessary action. She worked hard to understand herself better in therapy, and often announced that she was tired of being and acting like a victim. One day, she told us that in an argument with her boyfriend he'd accused her of giving off an aura of fragility, when it was really her way of shirking responsibility or refusing his requests. He had said to her, "You're saying to me, *'Look at how I've suffered; how can you expect any more from me?'* Then when I give up on you, you tell me I'm treating you like a child and that I'm trying to control you. What do you want from me?"

Insight Is Not Enough

There are those people who love to work on themselves and to keep changing. They crave the stimulation of the new and different. But we suspect that there are a lot more people like Cindy, Alana, and Kevin wanting to change, but battling resistance. Cindy's resistance emerged after she'd made a commitment to make a change. Kevin and Alana had to battle their resistance from the start. Their experiences validate the point that insight alone is not curative. We've watched many clients go through similar scenarios.

Cindy, Kevin, and Alana all made progress, in spite of their resistance. They didn't do it overnight, and they didn't get rid of their resistance completely, but they all moved forward, and so can you. You *can* overcome resistance and create the life you desire.

If one of the six keys has helped you to recognize the origins of your chronic dissatisfaction including its payoffs and its ultimate frustrations, you've done half the work already. But, now, you're going to have to battle your resistance to change. It is easy to decide to change but it's a difficult thing to do. It is the daily struggle that changing requires that defeats most people. You have insight. You have motivation. Then you come face to face with one of your old triggers and suddenly there's a moment of choice. Do you move forward, or do you fall back into old patterns?

This chapter is about the steps you can take to overcome your resistance.

> *Our dilemma is that we hate change, but we love it at the same time. What we want is for things to remain the same, but to get better.*
>
> —Sidney Harris

Seven Cornerstones for Creating Change

1. Realize That Your Best Thinking Got You Here

If your life isn't working the way you want it to, stop doing the same things over and over expecting a different result. Say "enough is enough," and mean it. If all your thinking and analyzing isn't getting you where you want to be, consider that more thinking and analyzing aren't going to help.

Your best thinking may be setting you up for continual disappointment. Do your thoughts allow you to recycle old family patterns of negativity, overgeneralizations, or scarcity? Then, "enough is enough."

Half the struggle with "never enough thinking" is the inflexible attitude of "*It should be enough; I shouldn't be having this problem; I wish something would just magically happen in my life to make me feel good about myself.*" If you don't have the life you desire, your very first step in learning how to be empathic with yourself is to admit that fact to yourself. Stop telling yourself you "should" be happy. Stop trying to count your blessings. As therapists we have met many clients who were beautiful and didn't believe it, intelligent but thought they weren't smart enough, successful but felt inadequate. Therapy would have been useless if we tried to convince them that they were all these things that they couldn't see.

One of our clients told us that in one of his quests for an answer to his malaise, he went to see a man who advertised himself as a spiritual guide. "He said to me, '*Son, you must learn to drink wine from an empty cup.*' You know, he hit the nail on the head, but not the way he thought. I'd spent my whole life looking for wine in empty cups! It was time to say, 'Okay, obviously the way I think I should go about things got me right here. Why not simply look for a glass that's full, instead of trying to make the best of what's empty?'" This may mean realizing that you have to give up on your own prescriptions for getting your needs met, admit that your ways aren't working, and take a leap of faith. That leap of faith may be to try something new that someone else suggested, or that you've heard about or read about. It may feel very uncomfortable. You may want to hold

on to your own thinking in a battle to be "right." But remember, being right and being happy can be two very different things.

2. Turn Your Problems into Possibilities

There's an old joke that goes: Two shoe salespeople were dispatched to a remote rural area. In just a few days, their employer received telegrams from each one. One read, "Get me out of here—no one here wears shoes." The other read, "Send more inventory—no one here owns shoes."

This story illustrates a great truth: It is not events that shape our experience so much as our personal "take" on those events. All of us view the world through the filters of values and beliefs we learned from our families and culture. It is critical that we become aware of these values and beliefs. With desire and determination you can take a second look at your personal "take" on reality and decide which values and beliefs serve you well and which are sabotaging your search for satisfaction.

Sam's Story

Sam, a forty-seven-year-old teacher, recalls an event that caused him to learn how to turn a seemingly unsolvable problem into an opportunity for personal transformation. "It was a day I had been waiting for most of my life, a true passage to adulthood, the purchase of my first house. Always one to be careful, I had visited the prospective house three times. I had checked every nook and cranny for possible problems. The owner seemed very honest and responsible. I was particularly impressed with all the built-in closet organizers on every floor. He seemed like a guy after my own heart. And the roof deck enchanted my wife.

"My most important concern had been to find a home in a quiet area. Every time I came back to visit this house, I listened for noise. I never heard any. I also asked the owner about noise. He told us, 'Occasionally you'll hear a little noise from the post office or during the garbage pickup. It's not a real problem.'

"We bought the house and moved in. Then, the nightmare began. The first morning in the new house my wife and I were startled awake by a mail delivery truck at six A.M. honking its way through the alley on its way to our next-door neighbor—the post office. In the next two days we learned that there were mail pickups and deliveries throughout the early morning hours. And if that wasn't bad enough, on the fourth day in the new house we were reawakened at six-thirty A.M. by the weekly garbage pickup truck, right outside our bedroom window.

"I was livid. How could I have missed all of this obvious noise? For the next month I was full of rage. This was my old pattern—Victim. I spent a lot of time yelling "I hate this place, we have to move!" and terrorizing my wife. After a month or two of complete rage, I began to look for solutions. I really didn't want to move, at least not right then. I loved the neighborhood and the house. My own best thinking had gotten me there. I thought that I should be able to get up at ten each morning, and the rest of the world should wait until then to go about its noisy business.

"My first attempt at a solution was to install the best sound insulation I could find on the windows. This worked marginally, at best. Next I bought a white noise machine to mask the noise. Still frustrated, I finally realized it was time for a major change, but this time, the change had to be within myself.

"My wife wasn't bothered at all. The early morning sounds woke her up, and she heard them as the sounds of city life, which she had been craving. She got up at six A.M. anyway. For years I thought of myself as a night person. Getting up before nine A.M. was a rare event. Yet over the years I had become aware that staying up late at night was leaving me tired and sluggish during the day. I had read Depak Chopra who said that if we get up around six A.M. and go to bed about ten P.M., optimal health would result. When I read that, I thought, 'That's nice for him, but I can't do that.' But I knew he was right. I just couldn't get motivated to change my sleep patterns.

"Then it finally hit me—this is the motivation! I was going to be awakened by the noisy mail trucks anyway, so why not get up by my own design and use the morning hours to my advantage? At first, I had good days and bad days. My plan was to get up at five-thirty (before the mail trucks arrived) and to work out. Initially, I had a lot of resistance. The entire transition took me about three months.

"Nowadays I have never felt better. Getting up earlier gives me more energy throughout the day and also helps me to fall asleep earlier and easier. And although there are still times the noise upsets me, I feel proud of my ability to take control and turn this problem around. I look back and realize a lot of wasted energy in my life was the result of being a late riser."

The following table shows how some other clients turned their problems into possibilities.

Problem	Possibility
1. My career is going well, my family life is good, if not perfect. But I still feel empty, as if I should do more or be more than I am.	1. Maybe all is not as well as I try to tell myself. Maybe there's a part of me that I haven't been able to express that could open up a whole new path for me.
2. My marriage is in deep trouble and has been for years. Do I leave or do I stay?	2. Whether I leave or stay, what can I learn about myself and how I interact in a relationship? Instead of blaming others, what can I say I really need that I'm not getting?
3. My mother's bout with cancer is ruining my life. I'm expected to be there for her constantly. I feel guilt, guilt, guilt. I'm a terrible daughter.	3. Is it possible that I can't be everything to everyone? Why do I need to feel terrible about myself to get motivated enough to call my mother? What's the message here?
4. I'm always on a plane, or in a taxi headed somewhere, always in motion. My wife is on my case for traveling so much.	4. What do I get from being away that I don't get from being home? What am I running from? What am I running to?

5. My friend Sally didn't return my phone call. I felt hurt and discounted. I generally withdraw and end relationships this way.	5. I could see this as a chance to practice my assertive communication skills and ask her why she didn't return my call. No matter what she says, I can view my call as personal growth and a validation of my feelings

3. Learn to Recognize the Moment of Choice

Kara, forty-two, was achieving the first career success she'd ever known since she'd left her job at an advertising agency to go off on her own, but she had a guilty secret that kept her from enjoying it. "I'd spend six hours at my computer pounding out ads, slogans, and schedules for media buys, the sun would start to go down, and more than anything else, I wanted a glass of wine."

But one glass of wine was turning into two and three. If the slogans didn't come easily, the ads seemed uninspired, or her clients called with negative feedback, the amount of wine consumed could turn into a whole bottle. For Kara, drinking wine at night seemed to be a soothing release. "I felt it helped me get up the nerve to be more creative. I created a number of ads when I was absolutely drunk that my clients loved."

Every morning Kara would wake up ashamed of how much she'd drunk the night before. "I knew I was playing with fire. I was becoming more and more successful, and I was drunk more and more often. Suddenly, people were respecting me. I had more business than ever, and one of my ads was actually up for an award. I didn't want to lose that. I didn't want to drink anymore, but the decision kept unmaking itself. Five-thirty P.M. would roll around and a voice would go off in my head: 'You don't really have a problem with alcohol. You couldn't accomplish so much if you did. You need it, just this once, to loosen up so you can get past this block. You deserve it.' Then I'd hate myself. With the life I wanted, drinking to the point of getting drunk every night didn't fit. But it was the only thing in the closet."

Kara recognized that 5:30 P.M. was her moment of choice. She could try to change her pattern. Or she could go to the convenience store for a bottle of wine. "I learned to call my husband at five-thirty to talk to him about my frustration that my ads weren't good enough, rather than drink to make the fear go away. Sometimes, when the workday was ending and five-thirty P.M. was looming, I would just get up and go to see a movie by myself to focus my mind on something else for a while. The voice in my head would say, 'If you stop drinking, you'll never have another creative thought in your life. You'll lose your ability to write. You'll never be the life of the party and make everyone laugh again.' That was resistance. Finally, I told myself, 'You can go back to drinking someday if that is really true. But you'll never know if you really need all this alcohol to be creative, unless you do without it for a while.'"

Kara isn't alone in finding that there's a certain time of day that makes her lose her resolve. Many of our clients have learned to recognize their moment of resistance—and the moment of choice that follows it. Look at your own patterns. When are you most likely to say, "What's the use?" When you have set a goal for yourself, and you don't

follow through, don't beat yourself up over it. That's probably a part of your habitual patterns. Instead, think about the specifics of how you resist change. Did you feel yourself give up at a specific moment? What was that moment? What happened and what did it mean? Don't just analyze—look for numbers.

If, like Kara, you find that you give up your plans for change at a specific time of day, think of how you can overcome your resistance now that you have that information. Kara found a lot of things she could do in the early evening to counter her wine drinking. First, she started going to movies to occupy her mind with something other than her craving. Now, her current favorite is walking to the coffee shop for a cappuccino. Whatever your issue is, you, too, can find ways to combat resistance once you can identify the times of day when it is strongest, or the people, places, or situations that are most likely to trigger it. When you know what your triggers are, you can figure out ways to break your old patterns and to challenge your resistance.

4. Empower Your Vision Instead of Your Problems

Dwelling on problems empowers those problems. Get into the habit of asking yourself: "Am I focusing more on the problem than on the solution?" A good rule of thumb is to spend about 20 percent of your time analyzing and understanding the problem and 80 percent of your time acting on the solution.

Gayle admits, "I married a man who excited me, stimulated me, challenged me, and often let me down. I learned a lot about why I was drawn to such a person in the first place. I had to do some work on myself if my marriage, barely six months old, was going to work. I spent hours on the phone with my sister, trashing him. My brother-in-law would also get on the phone and then we'd have a real trash fest, with a man's point of view as an added attraction. Boy, did he make me feel good! But I would feel really lousy the next day when I would realize that it was easy for my brother-in-law to tell me to move on and get a divorce, but that actually getting a divorce was going to be very hard for *me.*

"I realized that trashing my husband over the phone with my family wasn't going to help my situation at all. I had a lot of resistance about learning how to get along with another person and I had even more resistance to giving up some of my fantasies about marriage."

Gayle immediately began to feel better about her marriage when she began to concentrate on solutions rather than spending more time rehashing the problems.

5. Be Open to Help from Others

Not catering to resistance means that you must be open to asking for and accepting help. The idea that you don't need any help or support to make basic changes in your life is a trap. Although there are people who love the challenge of trying to get rid of old habits with new behavior, most people will resist change if they don't receive some coaching and support. We have met many people who haven't created the life they desire, because

they wouldn't reach out for help. They had friends who would have listened, provided support, money, and contacts. But they thought they could do it alone. Are you willing to ask for help? If not, why not? What's underneath your resistance? What good does it do you to go at it all alone?

Help can be as simple as making a phone call to a friend and saying, "I'm starting to forget why I'm trying to accomplish this, can you remind me?" One hallmark of successful people is their ability to absorb and use feedback from others. We all have blind spots when it comes to our personal habits and patterns. Consider the possibility that if you feel stuck in your life, it was "your best thinking" that got you there. Perhaps it's time for a new perspective.

In psychology, feedback is often referred to as "mirroring." This was discussed briefly in chapter 4. Essentially mirroring amounts to a reflection of how people see and experience you. Here are some examples of mirroring:

"Sally, I notice that you are always trying to take care of others. You seem to have trouble stating your own needs."

"Jane, you've been talking about having children for two years now; what's stopping you from discussing this with your husband?"

"Jim, whenever I give you feedback about how you backed down when you confronted someone, you get defensive."

6. Create Goals That Are Clear and Measurable

> *The reason most people don't reach their goals is that they don't define them, learn about them, or ever seriously consider them as believable or achievable.*
>
> —Denis Waitley

Resistance will easily get the best of you if your plans are sketchy, and your goals broad and unfocused. How can you create a plan of action that will discourage resistance? Try the following:

What, Why, and How

Begin with what, why, and how. First, decide exactly *what* you want (be clear and specific), write it down. Next, get clear on *why* you want each of these goals. Write down these reasons and share them with another person. It is important to remember that the stronger the why, the more assurance you will have of overcoming any resistance and achieving your goals. Last, write down specifically *how* you will achieve these goals. Include dates of completion. Plan to do something every day to move toward these goals.

Read these examples, and then create your own.

Example 1
What: My goal is to work out for thirty minutes three times this week.
Why: Because when I exercise I feel better, look better, and I have more energy.

How: I will go to the health club on Monday, Wednesday, and Friday mornings at 7:30 A.M.

Example 2

What: I will get up at 6:30 each morning.

Why: When I get up at a consistent early hour, I fall asleep more easily at night. I have more time to work and to play. I am more creative in the morning hours.

How: I will set my alarm every evening and commit to getting out of bed whether I feel like it or not. I will jump right into the shower.

Example 3

What: I will be more honest with my husband about my feelings.

Why: When I hold in my feelings, I tend to get depressed, anxious, or resentful. When I express myself I feel a sense of relief and heightened self-esteem.

How: I will find a mutually convenient time and ask him if I can talk about something personal. I will tell him I'm working on being more expressive so that I won't get depressed or anxious. I will use "I" statements and employ my other skills for more effective communication.

7. Give Change a Chance

It's not easy to change a pattern that may have persisted twenty or more years in your life. When you don't get results right away, you may think, "This isn't working, so why bother?" That's human. But those moments when your efforts at changing don't work offer opportunities to practice compassion and understanding for yourself. If change were an easy thing to do, everyone would do it. We would all be perfect beings.

Be persistent. Remember: You are doing the best you can. None of us wants to be miserable. When you fail to reach your goals, you often keep doing the same old things—only louder and harder. What you really need to do is to stop and learn what you are missing. Solving a problem will create relief for a day. Changing a pattern will create change for a lifetime.

Sometimes change doesn't bring us everything we thought it would. One of our clients lost 100 pounds. It took her two years, and she did it slowly and in a healthful way. "But I'm still depressed," she told us, astounded because she always thought that after losing weight she'd be happy. She admitted that she was beginning to think "What's the use?" again, the thought that had always been the precursor to a binge before she lost the weight.

This was an important moment for her to feel compassion and empathy for herself. She could always go back to her old eating habits that had put the weight on her in the first place. That would have been an easy thing to do. But why should she give up her hard-won weight loss so easily? Her goal became the desire to learn to live with her newly slim body in spite of occasional bouts of depression. She had to see what the future had in store for her. Perhaps this change in her weight wasn't the absolute antidote to depression, but what else could her thinner, healthier body bring into her life?

You, too, can work past your resistance and see what transpires. Change will be a lot more exciting than dwelling on your problems. It will be a lot more adventurous than

doing what you've always done. Working on changing will be much less boring than giving into your resistance and then arriving at the day when you say to yourself, "Why didn't I just take that risk? Why didn't I give myself a chance?" You can. You will. You can begin today. All you need is a little leap of faith and the knowledge that what we resist, persists.

> *The real voyage of discovery consists not in seeking*
> *new landscapes, but in having new eyes.*
>
> —Marcel Proust

9

Designing the Life of Your Dreams

Clarify and Realize Your Vision

*It's a funny thing about life; if you refuse to accept
anything but the best, you very often get it.*

—Somerset Maugham

There's an old proverb that reminds us, "If you don't know where you want to go, any road will take you there." If you could design your life just the way you'd want it, what would it look like? In this chapter you will focus not on what's missing, but on what can be created and how to do that.

This chapter is accompanied by the New Harbinger audiotape *Designing the Life of Your Dreams—A Guided Visualization*. The words and concepts found in these pages will engage the logical and analytical left hemisphere of your brain, while the guided visualization heard on the tape engages the creative and intuitive right hemisphere more fully. This type of right-brain engagement can stimulate a deeper connection with your emotions, creativity, and unconscious mind. In addition, the music on the tape can help you relax, dream, and enjoy your journey.

You will find that when you begin to empower your dreams, the world around you will begin to change. There are no limits to how you can design your life except for those you set in place with your own mind. To help you focus on specific goals now, you should take your own inventory on the *six key areas of satisfaction*. They are as follows:

The Six Key Areas of Satisfaction

1. Creating Health and Fitness

2. Creating Lasting Friendships

3. Creating Love

4. Creating Play and Adventure

5. Creating Meaningful Work and Financial Abundance

6. Creating a Satisfying Home

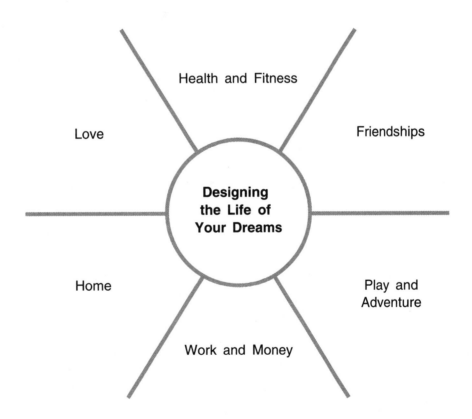

The Six Key Areas of Satisfaction Inventory

Take this short quiz to find out which areas in your life you want to develop. Read each statement and score each area from 1 to 10.

Questionnaire

	1–10
1. **Health and Fitness.** I take care of my body on a daily basis. I eat in a healthy manner and I exercise regularly to stay healthy and fit. I relax when needed.	
2. **Friendships.** I have good friendships. My friends and I support each other, spend meaningful time together, and have fun together.	
3. **Love.** I have an intimate partner with whom I share loving feelings. I am able to express my feelings openly. I feel satisfied in this area.	
4. **Play and Adventure.** Every week I make time for recreation, fun, adventure, and relaxation.	
5. **Work and Money.** I believe that my work is meaningful, and I feel confident in my ability to earn money, save money, and plan for my future financial needs.	
6. **Home.** I like where I live. This location fits in with my basic needs and values. Being in my house brings me a sense of peace and happiness.	

Scoring

A score of 1 means "I need to develop this area." A score of 10 means "I feel this area is no problem for me." Scores that fall in the middle mean that you've made progress toward your goal in that particular area and that you are moderately content.

Your Personal Growth Notebook

The pages that follow provide a personal growth notebook where you can record your thoughts and plan action steps while you are thinking about creating the life you desire. It's never too late to reopen the doors to your truest self. The key to creating and implementing a lasting vision is to continue clarifying the picture of your life. Allow yourself to "live" in the questions rather than "striving" for perfect answers.

For each area of personal growth, questions are provided to help you focus your thinking. Use these questions as a springboard, but don't let them limit you. Record your most adventurous, empowering thoughts in these pages. When you finish writing and

read back what you've written, you will find between those lines the life you desire and a blueprint for creating it.

Creating Fitness and Health

The first wealth is health.

—Ralph Waldo Emerson

1. Where do I have distress in my body? What might this be telling me?

_____

_____

_____

_____

_____

2. Do I eat in a healthy manner? What do I need to change?

_____

_____

_____

_____

_____

3. What kind of exercise works best for me? What are the ways of making my workouts more fun?

_____

_____

_____

_____

_____

_____

4. What am I willing to do this week, this month, to improve my health and fitness?

_____

_____

_____

_____

_____

_____

Freeing the body inevitably leads to freeing the heart.

—Gabrielle Roth

Creating Lasting Friendships

A friend is a gift you give yourself.

—Robert Louis Stevenson

1. Which of your friends or acquaintances would you like to spend more time with? Who would you like to spend less time with? Describe your ideal friend or social group. What kinds of people will nourish you with positive energy?

_____

_____

_____

_____

_____

_____

2. What might be getting in the way of your having the friendships you desire?

_____

_____

_____

_____

_____

_____

3. What activities would you like to initiate with your friends? Do you like to go to ball-games? Play cards? Would you like to have more meaningful conversations with the people you know?

_____

_____

_____

_____

_____

_____

4. How can you cultivate new friends? What groups, clubs, or activities would connect you with people who have similar interests? What one small step can you take this week to cultivate new friends?

_____

_____

_____

_____

_____

_____

A faithful friend is the medicine of life.

—Ecclesiasticus

Creating Love

Love is very simple; it is we who are complex.

—Leo Buscaglia

1. Describe the life mate you desire. What personality traits, values, or interests does that person have? What's *essential* as opposed to nice to have or "icing on the cake"?

_____

_____

_____

_____

_____

_____

2. What do you need to develop or change in yourself to create this type of relationship? Who do you need to be to attract the best mate for yourself?

_____

_____

_____

_____

_____

_____

3. Which people do you see as sources of love in the world? (These may be personal friends, mentors, or celebrities). How do they express their love?

_____

_____

_____

_____

_____

_____

4. In what ways can you be more loving today?

_____

_____

_____

_____

_____

_____

It is only with the heart that one can see rightly;
what is essential is invisible to the eye.

—Antoine De Saint-Exupéry

Creating Play and Adventure

All the animals except man know that the
principal business in life is to enjoy it.

—Samuel Butler

1. List ten activities that you enjoy doing.

_____

_____

_____

_____

_____

_____

2. What are five activities that you enjoyed doing as a child that you no longer do today?

_____

_____

_____

3. What's getting in the way of having more fun? How can you invest more energy in creating more fun for yourself?

4. What are you willing to do this week to create more adventure and play in your life? Who could be your partners in adventure?

Getting there isn't half the fun—it's all the fun.

—Robert Townsend

Creating Meaningful Work and Financial Abundance

1. What are your parents' beliefs about money? Are they based on scarcity or abundance? What did they do to make their beliefs apparent?

_____

_____

_____

_____

2. What are your beliefs about money? How does this manifest itself in your life?

_____

_____

_____

_____

3. What are your strengths in the area of work? How can you use these talents or skills to earn more money?

_____

_____

_____

_____

4. What specifically are you willing to do this week to further your goal of earning more money? This month? This year?

_____

_____

_____

_____

_____

_____

Money is the sixth sense which enables you
to enjoy the other five.

—W. Somerset Maugham

Creating a Satisfying Home

My special place. It's a place that no amount of hurt and anger
can deface. I put things back together there, it all falls right
in place—in my special place, my special place.

—Joni Mitchell

1. What are your favorite parts of your home and why?

_____

_____

_____

_____

_____

2. How can you make your home a place that brings you more joy and contentment?

_____

_____

_____

_____

_____

_____

3. Where would you really like to live and why?

_____

_____

_____

_____

_____

_____

4. What can you do this week to create the home you desire?

_____

_____

_____

_____

_____

_____

_____

Happiness is not having what you want but wanting what you have.

—Rabbi Hyman Schachtel

Choosing Goals

Now that you've done some exploration, it's time to choose one or two goals to begin designing the life you desire. Choose from any of the six areas. In the weeks that follow, continue creating goals until you have made measurable progress in designing the life you really want. (For a review of effective goal setting turn to chapter 5, "When You Can't Achieve the Success You Desire.")

Many people choose goals without having a firm conviction as to why that goal is important to them. The following exercise will help you to clarify your "why."

Your Personal Growth Goal—What, Why, and How

Examples

What is it? (E.g., *to have more fun in my life.*)

Why is it? (E.g., *I have always been a serious person and I tend to focus on work all the time. Planning some fun activities on a regular basis would give me more energy, lessen my tendency toward depression, and give me something pleasurable to look forward to each week. I think it would greatly improve the quality of my life.*)

How will you do it (action steps)?

1. Make a list of three activities that would be fun to do.

2. Choose one activity to schedule time for this week and do it.

3. Call a friend if necessary (e.g., a racquetball partner).

4. Make sure to build this into your weekly schedule.

> *He who begins too much accomplishes little.*
>
> —German Proverb

Your Personal Growth Goal

What is it?

_____

_____

_____

_____

_____

Why is it?

_____

_____

_____

_____

_____

_____

How will you do it (action steps)?

1. _____

2. _____

3. _____

4. _____

Remember: SMART goals are Specific, Measurable, Achievable, Realistic, and Timebound.

Staying on Track

> *Victory belongs to the most persevering.*
>
> —Napoleon Bonaparte

The Weekly Goal Assessment

Staying on track with your goals is best monitored within the time frame of one week. A weekly assessment helps you to keep an eye on the bigger picture without getting caught up in the details of the day.

Your Weekly Goal Sheet

Track your schedule for one week to see where your time goes. At the end of the week, try to quantify how much time you have spent pursuing the goals you identified as priorities earlier in this chapter.

	Monday	Tuesday	Wednesday	Thursday	Friday	Saturday	Sunday
6 A.M.							
7 A.M.							
8 A.M.							
9 A.M.							
10 A.M.							
11 A.M.							
12 Noon							
1 P.M.							
2 P.M.							
3 P.M.							
4 P.M.							
5 P.M.							
6 P.M.							
7 P.M.							

Managing Procrastination

One way to manage procrastination is to do the difficult things first. Start each day with the task you are most apt to avoid. We asked some of our clients what tasks they are most likely to avoid. Here are some of their answers:

- "I always avoid my bookkeeping. I let the bills pile up until I feel overwhelmed by the end of the month."

- "I procrastinate on cleaning up my office desk. The papers pile up and I feel disorganized throughout the day."

- "I never quite get around to planning my vacations. Maybe I secretly think that my free time is not that important."

- "I avoid my creative writing every day. I figure that I will get around to it later, but I never do."

Now it's your turn.

What Important Activities Do You Avoid?

1. _____

2. _____

3. _____

4. _____

5. _____

My Action Steps for Avoiding Procrastination This Week

1. _____

2. _____

3. _____

4. _____

5. _____

Increasing Your Motivation

Many people live life in a fog when it comes to their personal growth goals. We forget our New Year's resolutions by January 15. As the years melt together you may find that time goes by without any real change. The following exercise can be an excellent wake-up call.

1. Imagine your life five years from now, and you are in exactly the same place as you are today. How old are you? How will you feel?

_____

_____

_____

_____

2. Imagine your life ten years from now and you are in exactly the same place as you are today. How old are you? How will you feel?

_____

_____

_____

_____

3. Imagine your life twenty years from now and you are in exactly the same place as you are today. How old are you? How will you feel?

_____

_____

_____

_____

Monthly Goal Track Sheet

Some people have an easier time tracking their goals when they list them on a weekly basis and check them off when they have been met. You can use the following charts to track your goals, and after four weeks you will have a clear, concise picture of what you will have achieved.

Week #1: Date _____	
Goals (Be specific and time limited.)	**Completion**
1.	
2.	
3.	
4.	

Week #2: Date _____

Goals (Be specific and time limited.)	Completion
1.	
2.	
3.	
4.	

Week #3: Date _____

Goals (Be specific and time limited.)	Completion
1.	
2.	
3.	
4.	

Week #4: Date _____

Goals (Be specific and time limited.)	Completion
1.	
2.	
3.	
4.	

You miss one hundred percent of the shots you don't take.

—Wayne Gretsky

Some Thoughts for Your Journey

1. It is never too late to change. Every day is a new beginning.

2. You create your destiny. You are the author of your life.

3. Problems are opportunities for personal growth.

4. There are no mistakes, only lessons.

5. Take risks. Your fear will diminish when you confront it.

6. Take consistent and measurable action steps on your goals. Track them on a daily, weekly, and monthly basis.

7. Visualize your goals on a daily basis. Use affirmations to change those beliefs that are limiting.

8. Share your goals and desires with supportive and positive people. Share your progress and talk about your resistance.

9. Change usually takes place in small steps. As you go about creating the life you desire, take time to acknowledge small successes. Reward yourself and celebrate your achievements.

Remember that change is a journey. The six keys are your daily tools. We hope they will give you the energy and optimism to have a rewarding journey which results in you being able to create the life you desire.

Resources

*Audio Tapes and Compact Disks for Guided
Imagery and Relaxation*

Meditation

1. Emmett Miller. *Letting Go of Stress*
2. Salle Merrill-Redfield. *The Celestine Meditations and the Joy of Meditating*
3. Don Campbell. *Relaxation and Serenity*
4. Mitch Meyerson. *Songs for Serenity/A Path to Serenity*
5. Melody Beattie. *The Language of Letting Go* and *Lighting the Path*
6. John Bradshaw and Steven Halperin. *The 11th Step Meditation*
7. Louise Hay. *Meditations for Healing*
8. Patti Hall. *Warmth Within*
9. New Harbinger Audio. *Ten Minutes to Relax*
10. Bernie Siegal. *Reflections and Meditations*
11. Steven Halpern. *Comfort Zone*
12. Don Sepian. *Open Spaces*

Environmental Sounds

1. Gordon Hempton. *Earth's Morning Song*
2. Gordon Hempton. *Ebb and Flow*
3. Environments. *Psychologically Ultimate Seashore*
4. Legacy. *The Healing Sounds of Nature*
5. Ocean Music. *Northsound*

Suggested Reading

Beattie, Melody. 1990. *The Language of Letting Go*. San Francisco. Harper/Hazelden.

Bloomfield Harold. 1994. *How To Heal Depression*. Prelude Press: Los Angeles.

Bloomfield Harold. 1996. *The Power of Five*. Rodale.

Bourne, Edmund J. 1990. *The Anxiety and Phobia Workbook*. Oakland, CA: New Harbinger Publications.

Bradshaw, John. 1988. *Bradshaw on the Family*. Deerfield Beach, FL.: Health Communications Inc.

Cameron, Julia. 1992. *The Artist's Way*. New York: Tarcher.

Choquette, Sonia. 1997. *Your Heart's Desire*. New York: Three Rivers Press.

Covey, Stephan. 1989. *The Seven Habits of Highly Effective People*. New York: Simon and Schuster.

Dowling, Colette. 1988. *Perfect Women*. New York: Summit Books.

Gawain, Shakti. 1993. *The Path of Transformation*. Mill Valley: Nataraj Publishing.

Jampolski, Gerald. 1979. *Love Is Letting Go of Fear*. New York: Bantam Books.

Levinson, Jay Conrad. 1997. *The Way of the Guerilla*. New York: Houghton Mifflin.

McKay, Matt, and Pat Fanning. 1992. *Self-Esteem*. Oakland, CA: New Harbinger Publications.

Miller, Alice. 1981 *Drama of the Gifted Child*. New York: Basic Books.

Paul, Stephan. 1991. *Illuminations*. New York: HarperCollins.

Robbins, Anthony. 1994. *Giant Steps*. New York: Simon and Schuster.

Sills, Judith. 1993. *Excess Baggage*. New York: Viking.

Viorst, Judith. 1986. *Necessary Losses*. New York: Fawcett Crest.

Williamson, Marianne. 1992. *A Return to Love*. New York: HarperCollins.

References

Basch, Michael Franz. 1988. *Understanding Psychotherapy*. New York: Basic Books.

Bloomfield, Harold H. and Peter McWilliams. 1994. *How to Heal Depression*. Los Angeles: Prelude Press.

Borysenko, Joan. 1989. *Minding the Body, Mending the Mind*. New York: Bantam Books.

Bradshaw, John. 1988. *Healing the Shame That Binds You*. Deerfield Beach, FL: Health-Communications.

Copeland, Mary Ellen. 1992. *The Depression Workbook*. Oakland, CA: New Harbinger Publications.

Dowling, Collette. 1988. *Perfect Women*. New York: Summit Books.

Epstein, Mark. 1995. *Thought Without a Thinker*. New York: HarperCollins.

Fossum, Merle A. and Marilyn J. Mason. 1986. *Facing Shame*. New York: W. W. Norton.

Hanh, Thich Nhat. 1976. *The Miracle of Mindfulness*. Boston: Beacon Press.

McCallister, Frank. 1995. Private conversation.

Meyerson, Mitch and Laurie Ashner. 1996. *When Is Enough, Enough? What You Can Do If You Never Feel Satisfied*. Center City, MN: Hazeldon.

———. 1997. *When Parents Love Too Much*. Center City, MN: Hazelden

Peck, Scott. 1978. *The Road Less Traveled*. New York: Simon & Schuster.

Robbins, Tony. 1991. *Awaken the Giant Within*. New York: Simon & Schuster.

Williamson, Marianne. 1992. A Return to Love. New York: HarperCollins.

Some Other New Harbinger Self-Help Titles

Facing 30: Women Talk About Constructing a Real Life and Other Scary Rites of Passage, $12.95
The Worry Control Workbook, $15.95
Wanting What You Have: A Self-Discovery Workbook, $18.95
When Perfect Isn't Good Enough: Strategies for Coping with Perfectionism, $13.95
The Endometriosis Survival Guide, $13.95
Earning Your Own Respect: A Handbook of Personal Responsibility, $12.95
High on Stress: A Woman's Guide to Optimizing the Stress in Her Life, $13.95
Infidelity: A Survival Guide, $13.95
Stop Walking on Eggshells, $14.95
Consumer's Guide to Psychiatric Drugs, $16.95
The Fibromyalgia Advocate: Getting the Support You Need to Cope with Fibromyalgia and Myofascial Pain, $18.95
Healing Fear: New Approaches to Overcoming Anxiety, $16.95
Working Anger: Preventing and Resolving Conflict on the Job, $12.95
Sex Smart: How Your Childhood Shaped Your Sexual Life and What to Do About It, $14.95
You Can Free Yourself From Alcohol & Drugs, $13.95
Amongst Ourselves: A Self-Help Guide to Living with Dissociative Identity Disorder, $14.95
Healthy Living with Diabetes, $13.95
Dr. Carl Robinson's Basic Baby Care, $10.95
Better Boundaries: Owning and Treasuring Your Life, $13.95
Goodbye Good Girl, $12.95
Being, Belonging, Doing, $10.95
Thoughts & Feelings, Second Edition, $18.95
Depression: How It Happens, How It's Healed, $14.95
Trust After Trauma, $15.95
The Chemotherapy & Radiation Survival Guide, Second Edition, $14.95
Surviving Childhood Cancer, $12.95
The Headache & Neck Pain Workbook, $14.95
Perimenopause, $16.95
The Self-Forgiveness Handbook, $12.95
A Woman's Guide to Overcoming Sexual Fear and Pain, $14.95
Mind Over Malignancy, $12.95
Treating Panic Disorder and Agoraphobia, $44.95
Don't Take It Personally, $12.95
Becoming a Wise Parent For Your Grown Child, $12.95
Clear Your Past, Change Your Future, $13.95
Preparing for Surgery, $17.95
The Power of Two, $12.95
It's Not OK Anymore, $13.95
The Daily Relaxer, $12.95
The Body Image Workbook, $17.95
Living with ADD, $17.95
Taking the Anxiety Out of Taking Tests, $12.95
When Anger Hurts Your Kids, $12.95
The Addiction Workbook, $17.95
The Chronic Pain Control Workbook, Second Edition, $17.95
Fibromyalgia & Chronic Myofascial Pain Syndrome, $19.95
Flying Without Fear, $13.95
Kid Cooperation: How to Stop Yelling, Nagging & Pleading and Get Kids to Cooperate, $13.95
The Stop Smoking Workbook: Your Guide to Healthy Quitting, $17.95
Conquering Carpal Tunnel Syndrome and Other Repetitive Strain Injuries, $17.95
An End to Panic: Breakthrough Techniques for Overcoming Panic Disorder, Second Edition, $18.95
Letting Go of Anger: The 10 Most Common Anger Styles and What to Do About Them, $12.95
Messages: The Communication Skills Workbook, Second Edition, $15.95
Coping With Chronic Fatigue Syndrome: Nine Things You Can Do, $13.95
The Anxiety & Phobia Workbook, Second Edition, $18.95
The Relaxation & Stress Reduction Workbook, Fourth Edition, $17.95
Living Without Depression & Manic Depression: A Workbook for Maintaining Mood Stability, $18.95
Coping With Schizophrenia: A Guide For Families, $15.95
Visualization for Change, Second Edition, $15.95
Angry All the Time: An Emergency Guide to Anger Control, $12.95
Couple Skills: Making Your Relationship Work, $14.95
Self-Esteem, Second Edition, $13.95
I Can't Get Over It, A Handbook for Trauma Survivors, Second Edition, $16.95
Dying of Embarrassment: Help for Social Anxiety and Social Phobia, $13.95
The Depression Workbook: Living With Depression and Manic Depression, $17.95
Men & Grief: A Guide for Men Surviving the Death of a Loved One, $14.95
When Once Is Not Enough: Help for Obsessive Compulsives, $14.95
Beyond Grief: A Guide for Recovering from the Death of a Loved One, $14.95
Hypnosis for Change: A Manual of Proven Techniques, Third Edition, $15.95
When Anger Hurts, $13.95

Call **toll free, 1-800-748-6273,** to order. Have your Visa or Mastercard number ready. Or send a check for the titles you want to New Harbinger Publications, Inc., 5674 Shattuck Ave., Oakland, CA 94609. Include $3.80 for the first book and 75¢ for each additional book, to cover shipping and handling. (California residents please include appropriate sales tax.) Allow two to five weeks for delivery.

Prices subject to change without notice.